MORE THINGS YOU CAN DO WHEN YOU'RE DEAD

MORE THINGS YOU CAN DO WHEN YOU'RE DEAD

WHAT CAN YOU TRULY BELIEVE?

by

TRICIA J ROBERTSON

www.whitecrowbooks.com

For information, contact White Crow Books
at 3 Hova Villas, Hove, BN3 3DH United Kingdom,
or e-mail to info@whitecrowbooks.com.

For information, contact White Crow Books
at 3 Hova Villas, Hove, BN3 3 DH United Kingdom,
or e-mail to info@whitecrowbooks.com.

Cover Designed by Butterflyeffect
Interior design by Velin@Perseus-Design.com

Paperback ISBN 978-1-910121-44-3
eBook   ISBN 978-1-910121-45-0

Non Fiction / Body, Mind & Spirit / Death & Dying

www.whitecrowbooks.com

PRAISE FOR *MORE THINGS YOU CAN DO WHEN YOU'RE DEAD*

This remarkable book is one of the most reader-friendly accounts of life-after-death that has come my way. *More Things you can do When You're Dead* will entertain, inform, and perhaps infuriate those who read its accounts of reincarnation, mediumship, poltergeists, and the like. Tricia Robertson has done her homework even citing quantum physics as a possible way to fathom what serious researchers often call "the survival question." Especially enjoyable are the chapters on art and "automatic writing"; especially disturbing are the accounts of possession and exorcism. You may like it, you may hate it, but you will not be bored!

—Dr Stanley Krippner, author of many books on human consciousness including *Personal Mythology*

This book intrigues us further and surpasses the evidential and fascinating information given in Tricia's highly acclaimed book *Things you can do When You're Dead*. It follows on from book one by extrapolating certain topics and also providing strong evidence from other types of phenomena which strengthen the case for survival of human personality after physical death. It is again written in a clearly understandable, knowledgeable and down to earth manner, often with a tinge of humour, which makes it not only an informative but enjoyable read.

—Dr David Hamilton, author of many books including *It's the Thought that Counts* and *Is Your Life Mapped Out?*

Many scientists consider that we have now entered what is termed 'post-materialist science', which holds that mind is independent of matter and so can continue to exist after physical death. Empirical support for this view continues to accumulate, and Tricia Robertson's second book on *More things you can do When You're Dead* provides a lively and substantial service to post-materialist science by providing a massive range of evidence. She has had personal connections with much of it. Her conclusion seems justified in that the amount of evidence provided 'has demonstrated with court of law persuasion, that bodily death does not totally destroy human personality.' Her skills acquired as a teacher of mathematics and physics are put to good effect in presenting complex information in an ordered and attractive way. This is a very informative and enjoyable book that can be used as a handy reference.

—JOHN POYNTON, EMERITUS PROFESSOR OF BIOLOGY, UNIVERSITY OF NATAL, SOUTH AFRICA; SCIENTIFIC ASSOCIATE, THE NATURAL HISTORY MUSEUM, LONDON; PAST PRESIDENT OF THE SOCIETY FOR PSYCHICAL RESEARCH.

CONTENTS

To my little granddaughters, Caroline and Julia, for being such treasures, bringing love and light to the world and making me smile.

ACKNOWLEDGEMENTS

I acknowledge a great debt of gratitude to the hundreds, if not thousands, of responsible and intelligent psychical researchers from the past who are no longer with us. Without all of the fastidious groundwork covered, and data collected, by these keen researchers, I doubt if many people would take any of us at all seriously now. On a personal level I have to give thanks to all of the mediums and healers who gave freely of their time to work with me in experimental settings and all of the late 'greats' of psychical research that I have had the privilege to know and work with, such as David Fontana, Arthur Ellison, Monty Keen, Maurice Grosse and especially my late colleague, Professor Archie Roy. Archie was not only one of nature's gentlemen, extremely intelligent, correct in his working methods and courteous but also interested in everyone that he came into contact with. Only once have I ever known him to lose his temper with someone, and I am keeping that person's identity to myself! Let us just say that, surprisingly, it was not me.

FOREWORD

Tricia Robertson is a living treasure. In her 30 year career of investigating an astonishing variety of afterlife related phenomena she has gained experiences which, I daresay, are unique in this day and age. In her ground-breaking work with the P.R.I.S.M. (Psychical Research Involving Selected Mediums) Project she worked alongside some of the giants of modern afterlife research including Professor David Fontana, Professor Archie Roy, Montague Keen, Maurice Grosse, Professor Arthur Ellison and Guy Lyon Playfair. Her first hand experience of serious research into mediumship and her close friendships with some of the greatest modern paranormal researchers have given her a wonderful stock of experiences to draw on.

Tricia is also a wonderful story teller whose talents have been honed in tutoring for the Department of Continuing Education at Glasgow University and her many speaking engagements along with her radio, TV and internet interviews. She writes in a lovely humorous conversational tone which makes this, her second book in this series, as easy to read and as engaging as the first. Because of this the book is ideal for people who are new to the field and want to know whether there has been any serious scientific investigation of the greatest question any human being can ask, what is going to happen to me when I die?

Tricia covers a huge variety of experiences, many of which are frequently encountered and debated in the real world. Her chapters on earthbound spirits, poltergeists, apparitions, obsession and possession will be of great interest to those interested in hauntings and things that go bump in the night. Her personal experiences in regard to these phenomena give great insight into the reality of being a paranormal investigator since she was often called to cases as part of her work as a council member, past Vice President and Immediate Past President of the Scottish Society for Psychical Research.

Of special interest is her chapter on Paranormal Healing in which she outlines case studies that she has personally collected during a five year study of two modern healers, Gary Mannion and Nina Knowland. Instead of reading like a dry scientific paper these studies are full of the life and personality of the patients, their surprise that spiritual healing worked for them, and of her own interactions with them during follow up interviews.

This book is mostly based on first hand experiences – either of Tricia herself or of people whose integrity and judgement she had come to trust – the value of which can never be over-estimated. As Tricia herself writes "I have to stress that there is no substitute for personal experience in any avenue of paranormal enquiry but maybe we can glean the flavour of the experiences if we imagine ourselves actually being there and seeing them for ourselves." Recording in book form many of these insights has been a great contribution to the field of psychical research. I was especially glad to see her accounts – by people who sat with brilliant physical mediums, like Gordon Higginson and Rita Goold – which I had not seen published elsewhere.

As Tricia points out, those who debunk the paranormal seldom have field experience and are restricted to sitting in an armchair speculating on how fraud might have been carried out and how they themselves might have been able to discover the fraud if only they had been called in to investigate. Of course this is not evidence. It is not science. It is pure prejudice.

This book is compelling reading and will be of great interest to anyone who wants to know about just some of the things you *can* do when you are dead!

Victor Zammit, Retired lawyer, afterlife investigator, and author
of *A Lawyer Presents the Evidence for the Afterlife*

INTRODUCTION

Does our personality, our essence, whatever makes us, 'us', survive after the demise of the physical body and are we in fact in possession of strange talents and abilities that cannot be understood while we are still alive? These are among the questions I hope to address within this book.

Do phenomena, such as apparitions, poltergeist activity, mediumship, obsession, possession, automatic writing, psychic art, materialisation and reincarnation actually exist? In my experience, they certainly do.

If you are looking for a quick description of this book, it would be that it takes a common sense look at and an examination of claims of paranormal phenomena, especially evidence for life after death. There is plenty of evidence 'out there' if you know where to look. So what is the evidence and where can we look for it? This book will demonstrate that educated people of high intelligence have taken these matters very seriously for more than one hundred years, and they still do so. Popular paranormal movies and hyped up TV series do not do anyone any favours, – unless, of course, you want to scare yourself witless for the evening.

This is not a dry and dusty tome as it deals with real-life situations – and where there are people there is also emotion and, at times, humour. This is reality – this is what actually happens. I am not trivialising the subject of life after death, but merely making it 'normal', as indeed it is.

This book is written for those ordinary people in the street who just do not know what to believe or what evidence they can rely on in these matters. After thirty years of research, I share more of my experiences with you within the contents of this book. Everything I have written is expressed with 100% honesty and from a very grounded stance.

Many people feel that they have been contacted by those who have departed this mortal existence. The methods of contact indeed vary from a minor intrusion upon the recipient to, on a rare occasion, perceived terror.

These methods of contact may include:-

The aroma of a person, perhaps their particular perfume, pipe tobacco, and so on – something that was associated with the deceased.

Interference with electrical goods.

A feeling of chill in the air, or the hairs standing up on your arms.

Seeing an apparition.

Receiving a telephone message from someone departed.

Receiving a computer or mobile phone message from someone who has passed over.

Hearing a radio or TV message spoken with the voice of a deceased person.

A feeling of being touched – normally a brush on the cheek or on your hair.

Some poltergeist activity, where there is meaningful movement of objects for attention.

Hearing a spontaneous direct voice.

Receiving an evidential message through a medium.

Gaining information from sitting in a circle - either mental or physical.

Witnessing materialisation within a circle.

Having a Near-Death Experience, during which you have met a deceased person.

Experiencing a premonitory dream.

Being able to produce inspired automatic writing.

Receiving a miraculous healing.

These are just some of the things that people appear to be able to instigate and manipulate after they have died - in fact 'Things they can do when they're dead', even if it is just influencing those still alive through inspiration.

People often seek after-death communication from a loved one through mediums, but this is not the only way to look at these matters and, sadly, not all mediums are necessarily good mediums. This is where psychical research comes in. We can approach the subject of survival from many angles and thus, hopefully, provide a clearer and bigger picture of what may, or may not, be going on.

There is no doubt that good mediums do a wonderful job for people who are bereaved but, as I said, not all mediums are necessarily responsible or good mediums.

Some of the material in this book is mindboggling and often stretches limits of credibility, but nevertheless the material is accurate.

I have experienced plenty of mind-expanding phenomena in my 33 years as an active psychical researcher. Let me tell you about them.

Chapter 1

BACKGROUND

The metered, rational study of paranormal phenomena is usually called psychical research. One problem with psychical research is *not* that examples of phenomena are difficult to find and describe, but that the range of topics one can study is vast. When these matters are studied in a University setting they are usually under the banner of the Psychology Department and the term used for such laboratory methodological studies of any particular phenomenon is Parapsychology. In my opinion, if research into these matters was carried out by other university departments, the subject could just as easily be called Para-physics or Para-biology. However, there has been an enormous amount of valuable experimentation carried out under the banner of parapsychology in Universities throughout the world resulting in a prolific output of data. I could not even estimate the number of papers and presentations that must have been made throughout the years. The J. B. Rhine laboratory alone must have collected an enormous database of experimental results.

Professor Ian Stevenson, several years ago, headed a unit in the University of Virginia which studied, and still studies, claims of reincarnation from children who, from when they can speak, remember a previous life. To the best of my knowledge they have collected well over 3,000 cases for study and analysis. Science gathers information, compiles databases, and considers the information collected for any supportive evidence and common factors that could lead to tentative hypotheses.

Those of us who work 'in the field', going out and about to study things that happen to people in real life situations, have added factors to consider. Indeed some of these factors *can* be *psychological,* but that is by no means the full story. We also gather and assimilate information and evidence on any particular topic, record any suitable data, check out witness testimony and also try to formulate a theory which fits all of the facts.

The most important part in the last sentence is 'a theory which fits *all* of the facts'.

Many avid vocal critics of psychical research cherry-pick the information that they wish to speak about in public, thus avoiding material which may not fit into their world model at that time. Many adopt the attitude that certain things just cannot happen; therefore there must be a flaw in the examination of a particular case. They also seem to adopt the attitude that if *they* had investigated that case they would have found out just where the investigator had gone wrong. They often postulate but do not provide any actual evidence to show where a particular researcher has gone wrong.

Psychical researchers have to be extra vigilant in their work as we have everybody, more or less, against us, squashing us from either side. Some scientists feel that we know all of the laws of physics and that paranormal phenomena just do not conform to any of them, therefore there must be an error in the findings. They have established and accepted a fixed paradigm which suits them. Deeply religious people feel that we may be upsetting their ideas of God, Heaven and Hell, etc.

Neither of these ideas are correct. Paranormal phenomena operate in a manner unknown to us at this time. Once the modus operandi is eventually understood the phenomena will not be paranormal, but understandably normal. As far as religion is concerned the findings of psychical research, especially in survival issues, should add evidence to the belief that there is life after death.

Any book or article relating to paranormal phenomena, or the survival of human personality after death, can often suffer badly from the criticisms of people who have extreme bias, or who have no experience whatever in these matters but who still persist in giving their opinion anyway.

There is a principle which is a bar against all information, which is proof against arguments and which cannot fail to keep a man in everlasting ignorance – that principle is contempt prior to investigation. —Herbert Spencer

We all know that people can exaggerate or misperceive experiences and that some people can be very fanciful, but these are not the type of examples that I will be dealing with in this book. As I said, the contents of this book are written with 100% honesty on my part and my only motive is to share my experiences with those people who have not had the same opportunities to examine these matters.

In my last book, *Things You Can Do When You're Dead*, I made a cursory reference to the setting up of the Society for Psychical Research (S.P.R) in London in 1882. The circumstances which brought this about were very interesting. The general idea was that the S.P.R. would form a cohesive approach to the study of all things allegedly paranormal in as scientific a manner as possible.

Professor William Barrett called a conference of people who might be interested in such a Society. It was held on the fifth and sixth of January, 1882 at 38 Great Russell Street, London, in a Spiritualists' Meeting House. The creation of a society was proposed and a steering committee was formed which met at Hensleigh Wedgwood's house on the seventh and the ninth of January. On February 20th, the conference was re-convened and the Society for Psychical Research was formally constituted. Henry Sidgwick reluctantly agreed to be President.

Barrett was also involved in the creation of a Society with similar motivation in the United States in January 1885. During a tour there in 1884 he had aroused the interest of a number of educated people and the American Society for Psychical Research, A.S.P.R. was founded with the astronomer Simon Newcomb as President. William James, arguably the best psychologist the United States has ever produced, became its leading light.

The foundation of the Society for Psychical Research in London in 1882 consolidated the desire for a systematic study of various aspects of phenomena. Although many serious scientists were involved in the set-up of the SPR, it might surprise and interest you to see the composition of the original council.

In his paper on the Founders of the S.P.R., Fraser Nicol points out how the myth arose that the Society for Psychical Research was *'founded by a group of scholars and scientists.'* In fact the composition of the first Council was 68 per cent spiritualist; spiritualists were elected as honorary secretary and honorary treasurer and, in the original list of members of the Society, there were more spiritualists than scholars and scientists. There would therefore have been equal truth in a myth that the S.P.R. was founded by a group of Spiritualists! That council consisted as follows.

Spiritualists	Non-Spiritualists
W. F. Barrett, physicist	Walter R. Browne, civil engineer
E. T. Bennett, hotel keeper	Edmund Gurney, Scholar
Mrs George Boole, author	F. W. H.Myers, scholar and poet
Alexander Calder, business man	Frank Podmore, civil servant
Walter H. Coffin, scientist	J. Lockhart Robertson, alienist
D.G.Fitzgerald, telegraphy expert	Henry Sidgwick, philosopher
C. C. Massey, barrister	
Rev. W. Stainton Moses, schoolmaster	
F. W. Percival, scholar	
Edmund Dawson Rogers, journalist	
Morrell Theobald, accountant	
Hensleigh Wedgwood, philologist	
George Wyld, physician	

Mrs George Boole was the widow of a mathematician. She resigned from Council in September 1882, being uncomfortable that she was the only woman on it. The other members classified as spiritualists were all educated men, many of them following professions. The Rev. W. Stainton Moses was not only a schoolmaster but was himself a noted psychic. On the non-spiritualist list were four Fellows or former Fellows of Trinity College, Cambridge – Browne, Gurney, Myers and Sidgwick.

Six committees were set up by the first Council to investigate thought-reading, mesmerism, Reichenbach phenomena, apparitions and haunted houses, spontaneous experiences and physical medium-ship. Reichenbach was a well-respected German chemist, who had the scientific temerity to investigate a girl who claimed that she could actually see the magnetic field around a magnet. He carried out a number of blind experiments with her and concluded that her claims appeared to be real. Other scientists of the time then took a step back from him because, naturally, they knew better!

By any standards, the Society's work in psychical research in the following thirty years was astonishingly high in quality and quantity.

Several major investigations resulted in publications that have withstood the test of time. The Proceedings of the Society for Psychical Research in those years contained reams of documentation/articles/ written experimental data of the very highest order. The effective workers in the Society were all young or early middle-aged. When the Society was formed, the oldest was Sidgwick, aged 43. The ages of the others were: Barrett 38, Gurney 34, Hodgson 26, Myers 39, Pease (a friend of Podmore who took part in investigations) 24, Podmore 26, Mrs Henry Sidgwick 36. Oliver Lodge joined the Society at the age of 32. The average age was 33. I feel that we need to get back to intellect, youth and enthusiasm in these matters.

Apropos the study of these matters, I contend that whatever the topic under examination, the phenomenon can be attributed to one of four things.

Human source

External source

Fraud

Delusion: which includes misperception, or poor recollection of events

Let us apply this thought to various phenomena, while remembering not to prejudge any particular topic before reading the relevant chapter.

Do you know what we call opinion in the absence of evidence? We call it prejudice.

—MICHAEL CRICHTON

Chapter 2

MATERIALISATION

In my last book I dealt fairly comprehensively with the topic of 'Apparitions', where a person reports seeing a 'ghost'. I wish now to continue along this avenue by looking at the phenomenon of materialisation. Common to both of these phenomena is the fact that the human figure of a deceased person is visible, or partly visible, and witnessed by a percipient or percipients.

Whereas an apparition may be reported under a variety of situations, materialisation is a phenomenon that usually takes place within a séance. There are many reported historical examples of this; perhaps the best known through the work of Sir William Crookes, the eminent British physicist and chemist, who sat in a 'circle' which was run by a Miss Florence Cook. In this circle it was recorded that the medium, Cook, would go into an altered state of consciousness and subsequently a white substance would emerge from her body and build up into separate individual recognisable figures, which could then walk around the room and communicate with some of the sitters. This white smoky substance was given the name 'ectoplasm'. It could have been called anything – quantum smoking, or anything else – the name is unimportant. One of the regularly materialised figures was of a woman who called herself Katie King. This figure was not hooded, therefore could be seen clearly, and was obviously taller than the medium. It was also noted that, unlike the medium, she had longish finger nails; the medium's being considerably shorter. Mrs Crookes attended these meetings with her husband, along with other sitters. Crookes himself examined and tested the situation to the best of his ability. He even took photographs of the whole proceedings while the electric light was switched on. After time consuming, rigorous examination of this circle he eventually concluded that he could find no fault in the proceedings and that the phenomenon of materialisation was genuine in this case.

One difference between a materialised figure and a spontaneous apparition is that within a circle situation people are *hoping* to see the figure of a departed person, but when faced with a spontaneous apparition – that is quite a different matter. Surprise and fear often enter this scenario. Another idea to consider, of course, would be that the method of creating a spontaneous apparition may not have anything to do with the 'ectoplasm' produced within a séance and therefore some other modus operandi may be at work.

I personally know about an occasion in 1975, where the English medium Gordon Higginson held a materialisation séance in the hall of The Glasgow Association of Spiritualists. Unfortunately this was about seven years before I began to take an interest in these matters, but I have written and verbal testimony from several trustworthy people who were there.

This hall holds just over 200 people. There were, and still are, blackout curtains suspended by means of ordinary curtain rails on the large windows. Because of this, the blackout was by no means complete and tiny shards of light came around the edges of the curtains during the demonstration. Gordon Higginson was seated in a chair on the slightly raised platform that is in situ at that location within a flimsy wooden cabinet which was covered with black material, like a curtain.

One woman, Diane Mitchell, who subsequently became a good friend of mine, attended that event. It was one of her first ventures into these matters. She was very suspicious of the whole thing and thought to herself, 'If this is a fraud, I'm going to get to the bottom of it.' With this in mind she arrived very early and managed to occupy a seat in the front row, right in the middle, where her eye-line was focused on the edge of the platform and hence in line with the bottom of the medium's chair which was a few feet away.

The proceedings began, with a full capacity of around 200.

After introductions and a period where the medium settled in to his chair, the front of the cabinet was covered by the black material.

Diane's eyes were glued to the foot of that cabinet. All lights were now switched off. After a short time she saw what looked like a substance resembling white smoke billowing out from under the black curtain. She was still somewhat sceptical. This scepticism somewhat diminished when the white smoke spilled out onto the platform from under the curtain, and then gradually built up into the shape of a man. The figure seemed to have a self-illuminating quality and was not just any man, but her father...she was stunned. Even more so when it moved towards her and said, 'Where's Doris?' This was her mother's name. More than somewhat taken aback she managed to blurt out a response to that question and further questions and statements that followed... no doubt with her in a slight state of shock.

Every person in the room could see that figure and all subsequent figures from the correct perspective of their seated positions in the room. At one point in the proceedings, a person who was seated on the platform at the side of the cabinet leaned over and pulled the curtain aside so that everyone could see the medium in the chair. They all saw the medium, Gordon, slumped in the chair with this white smoky substance emanating from various parts of his body.

Recipient after recipient received information from, or had a conversation with, a relevant materialised figure who demonstrated meaningful personal knowledge about their individual lives.

The proceedings lasted for about an hour and a half, where, in plain sight, figure after figure seemed to disappear and then another figure built up for the next recipient.

One of the psychologically strange things that happened after that was that about two weeks later, when cognitive dissonance had set in, Diane managed to convince herself that these events could not have happened. On further personal interrogation she then intellectualised and realised that those events *did* happen and, being an intelligent person, had then to integrate them into her world model; her new paradigm. Avoiding change in our thinking and absorption of new facts is actually something that we all tend to do as no one likes to alter their personal understanding or conception of reality.

Since 200 people witnessed the same proceedings that evening I think that we can rule out misperception or fraud in this case.

Margaret Falconer

The following is a personal account from the respected and wonderful Scottish medium, Mrs Margaret Falconer. It describes another séance at which the medium was, once again, Mr Gordon Higginson.

Here is my experience of a wonderful week at Stansted.

Arriving at Stansted we were given the keys to room 208 which I was sharing with three other people, my mum, Jean and Iris. We had hired a bus and it was a long drive from Arbroath to Stansted, so you can imagine how tired we were and we wanted to go to bed early. But our Jean, an older lady who was so full of mischief, decided to play tricks and she pinned my nightdress at the neck so that I could not get it over my head. In retaliation, when she went for a bath I pinned her sheets to her bed. When she came back into the room the sight that met us was something to behold; she wore a shower cap, had removed her false teeth and wore a see-through nightdress and an old cardigan on top with holes in the sleeves. She also sported knee bandages. The laughter was so loud and raucous that I jokingly said that Coo Coo, Gordon Higginson's guide, would be watching us and Jean said, 'Don't be stupid.' On the Monday evening there was a physical séance scheduled in the library, which meant that during the day we were not allowed into the room as it needed to be cleaned and free from dust. We had to meet outside the library at 7.30pm and were not allowed to take handbags in. Before we entered the room Gordon asked if we could choose two people to search him in order to prove that he was not carrying anything on his person and we accordingly chose two men, both of whom were openly very sceptical. While we waited, an older lady, of very strong character, said, 'I hope my husband comes tonight as I have waited 15 years for a contact from him.' We all wished the best for her and hoped he would come. Charles Sherrit let us into the room and the séance began. Gordon was sitting within a wooden cabinet, which was covered by a black curtain and he went in to a trance. The first communicator who came through was Coo Coo who said she had visited room 208 on Saturday night and they were having great fun. She then described everything that happened, right down to Jean's night attire, leaving us all, including Jean, dumfounded. We had never seen her so quiet or lost for words. Next we heard an old man's voice and this was in a broad Arbroath dialect. He said, 'Wilma I am here.' This turned out to be one of the ladies in our group who was raised by her grandparents, but we only knew her as Fiona and never realised that her name was actually Wilma. Her granddad said, 'I still go for a game of dominos to the 'Ploo and Hara', meaning the Plough and Harrow. The next voice was of a young man, again with an Arbroath accent, who said, 'Ma it's me, Stuart, please don't go back to the cemetery, I'm no there. It was very nice of you to put that wreath of flowers in the shape of a motorbike on my grave for my 21st birthday, but it's a waste of money because I am here around you.' He then said, 'I will ask if I can bring you a flower from spirit' and a beautiful white carnation was apported...it was as if it appeared out of thin air. Then it felt as if the energy had changed around Gordon and the curtain was pulled back from the cabinet for the rest of the séance. A mist appeared (ectoplasm) from, and around the medium, and a small man began to materialise. You could see his features very clearly and the old woman in the room shouted, 'Harry you have come at last!' He answered by saying, 'Yes and I won't be back again, I was under your thumb all our married life but I want you to know I am happy in spirit.' The old woman replied, 'I know I was hard on you and I am sorry, but I am happy to know that you are happy in the spirit world.' The ectoplasm then started to disappear and a few other messages were given, then Coo Coo's voice came back through the air: she told us that she had been back to room 208 and had let Jason the cat in. In addition she informed us that she had also emptied out the contents of one lady's handbag. She added that she had torn a page out of an address book and maybe one day she would give it back. Coo Coo then said, 'I have brought a present from that bedroom for the ladies'.... and the safety pins that were previously pinned to my nightdress just appeared in my hand. Needless to say when the séance finished we all rushed to room 208. The room was very cold and Jason the cat was on my bed. (I hate cats) The contents of my bag were thrown around him and whenever we tried to get him off the bed he would hiss and spit. After an hour he gently got up and meowed to get out of the room. We had a wonderful week, filled with many thought provoking memories.'

Author's note: she never did get the page out of the address book back.

I understand that Gordon Higginson demonstrated this type of materialisation for many, many, years throughout the UK. If he was the only person ever to do this then we might think it very strange and perhaps a little suspect, but he was not and to this day he is certainly not.

There was a private circle, not so many years ago, which used to meet in the north of England. The medium in that circle was Mrs Rita Goold.

My late colleague, Professor Archie Roy, attended that circle on more than one occasion. As well as being an Emeritus Professor of Astronomy at the University of Glasgow Archie also ran NATO advanced study seminars throughout the world and was invited, on more than one occasion, to speak to delegates at American Space Centres. My point is that he was nobody's fool.

This circle operated mostly in the dark, but they were allowed to hold torches with red paper over the bulb and when given the word from the medium, they were allowed to turn the torch on, thus shining a red light into the room. Archie would testify to the fact that on more than one occasion he was allowed to shine his torch onto the face of a materialised, smiling small boy who stood right in front of him. Archie's hand would then be taken and the red light directed downwards as the child said, 'See me wiggle my toes' and there, sure enough, were the bare feet of a child with toes eagerly wiggling. Another phenomenon that Archie has witnessed, on many an occasion, was that when he was sitting on a sofa and the medium said that Helen Duncan was coming, he would feel the sofa give a huge jolt as the weight of a fairly heavy person plonked down beside him. She would then have a conversation with him during which she would repeat from time to time, 'Ye ken whit I mean Archie.' This was usually accompanied by a fairly forceful slap on the upper arm. Archie told me that he was sure that he would have bruises on his arm when he got home.....but surprisingly he didn't. To support this claim, I have tape recordings of some of the proceedings within that circle. Therefore if Archie along with the other sitters had imagined the events, so did the tape recorder. Along with this I have a tape from another circle, given to me by the medium Mary Armour, in which Helen Duncan purports to come through via direct voice. I have to say that the tone, phrasing and inflections in this voice on the tape are very similar to the voice in the Goold circle. As the tape recordings are a hard fact, we can rule out misperception or poor memory, after the fact, as an explanation for these phenomena. As a point if interest, Rita Goold is a very slightly made woman, unlike Helen Duncan, and, as far as I know, she never took a penny from the sitters at any séance.

Michael Roll

The following is another account of the Rita Goold circle, written by a gentleman called Michael Roll.

The Experimental Proof of Survival After Death

'I can be absolutely precise about the day that changed my life forever. It was September 4, 1982.

This is the day I read in the *Psychic News* that a revolutionary scientific experiment had taken place. A journalist, Alan Cleaver, had carried out a very simple scientific exercise that proved, beyond any shadow of doubt, that we all survive the death of our physical bodies, and that we are all eventually reunited with our loved ones who have passed over before us.

This proof is just as comprehensive as the day, two thousand three hundred years ago, that the Greek scientist, Eratosthenes, proved that the world is round and not flat.

The investigative journalist, Alan Cleaver, had come across what I had been seeking ever since my mother had told me about a series of scientific experiments that had been carried out by Sir William Crookes in 1874. Crookes published the results of these experiments in The *Quarterly Journal of Science*. He had carried out these experiments with what is known as a materialisation medium. This type of medium does not just give evidence of survival after death like a mental medium; they are able to provide the scientific proof, where all five of our senses are working, where repeatable experiments under laboratory conditions can be carried out. Materialisation mediums carry out the same functions as a telescope or a microscope. They bring into focus something that we can't normally see. The human mind and brain are far more sophisticated instruments than anything invented by human beings on Earth.

The only thing missing from the Crookes experiments was that the "dead" person, Katie King, who materialised at his experiments, had passed over so long ago that he was unable to reunite Katie with her close relations who were still on Earth.

This is where Alan Cleaver steps in. At his experiments with the materialisation medium Rita Goold, he was able to carry out the scientific exercise that Crookes was unable to do. Rita Goold had six recently deceased people materialising every time she gave a demonstration. One of these was the materialisation medium Helen Duncan who was killed in 1956 as the result of a police raid.

A meeting was set up for Helen Duncan to be physically reunited with her daughter on Earth, Gena Brealey. Thanks to the Internet, every reader can now go to their computer and read Alan Cleaver's full report.

Six months later a friend of mine, Alan Crossley, who knew Helen Duncan very well, also took part in another scientific experiment where he was able to talk about things that only he and the "dead" Helen knew. Alan Crossley also then went through exactly the same experience as Sir William Crookes. He was physically reunited with his wife who had passed over four years previously.[1]

Following this, I made contact with Rita Goold and she kindly invited me to take part in her experiments. All the "dead" people who were materialising were as solid and as natural as we are. I was physically reunited with my father in March 1983. He passed over in 1967. From this moment on I have spent the rest of my life telling as many people as possible that it is a stone-cold scientific fact that losing a loved one is only a temporary tragedy. The full story can now be seen by every person on Earth who has access to a computer.

I pressed Michael Roll, author of the preceding narrative, for a more personal account of this circle and he favoured me with the following.

'Tricia, I wanted to concentrate on the proof of survival that materialisation mediums are able to provide. This is the reason why I featured the one hour talk that Gena Brealey had with her "dead" mother Helen Duncan.

---

[1] Reference: *Psychic News*, February 26, 1983. *Crookes and the Spirit World* (1972) Souvenir Press.

My father was a discarnate guest at the experiment but could not communicate like Helen had learnt to do over a number of years. At my first visit to Leicester, at the end of the experiment, the materialised Russell Byrne said, "You are coming back next week with your mother Michael. Is there anybody over here you would like us to get?" I said I would love to meet my father who passed over in 1967. Russell replied, "If he is over here we will try and dig him out."

Sure enough, the following week Helen Duncan said that they had a lovely surprise for me; they had my father with them. She took hold of my hands and said, "It is important that you do not touch your father because he has not learnt to materialise like some have done over a number of years. He can touch you but you must not touch him."

First of all Dad went over to my mother and apologised to her for his behaviour to her while on Earth. Dad was a poor husband but a good dad to me. Then he came to me with his earthly smells, heavy smoker and beer drinker. He then patted me on the head. This is what he did while on Earth, sometimes in front of my mates, which embarrassed me. My father was a former professional cricketer and a member of the MCC. My son Lawson was two when dad died. I said to my father, "What do you think of Lawson coming out to bat at Lords for England under 19's and playing for Gloucestershire against Sri Lanka a few months ago?" Dad and I were completely overcome with emotion and frustration. Helen Duncan then stepped in and said, "Now Harry, you can't just turn up and communicate like we have learnt to do over a long time."

I was in such a state that I was not thinking like a scientist. What I should have done for my report to Professor Archie Roy was to ask Helen to translate. I should have asked Helen to ask Dad to name all his best friends on Earth. However this scientific exercise took place a few days later when I was at home in Bristol. The phone rang and it was a mental medium from Woking. She said that she had my father with her. I told her that I am very sceptical about this sort of thing but if she can get Dad to name all his close friends when he was on Earth then this would prove that she did have my father with her. This she did, full names and sometimes where they worked. She even got friends whom Dad met in Australia, including the great wicket keeper Bert Oldfield.

However, she did not name my father's best friend, the one I was concentrating on like mad. This proved to me that this had nothing to do with mind reading.

You can of course use all this if you want to. It will be great for my grandchildren to read later in life.

You can see why I am working so hard to let people throughout the world have the peace of mind that I enjoy. Everybody on Earth should have this knowledge that losing a loved one is only a temporary tragedy, that dying is just the start of a tremendous adventure. But most of all that we are all personally responsible and liable for all our thoughts and actions while we are plugged into our physical body, which is only a space suit for our short stay on Earth. When the space suit packs in we go back to where we came from. If this was understood, people would start to leave happiness in their wake instead of misery.'

Michael also reminded me that John Logie Baird speaks of materialisation in his memoirs *Sermons, Soap and Television,* Autobiographical Notes published by the Royal Television Society in 1988.

On page 66 Baird tells how a scientific friend of his, a distinguished professor of entomology, carried out an experiment with a materialisation medium. He took the finger prints of the materialised person and, when checked, they were identical to those on the record of the dead person. Michael states that this is crushing proof of survival and that this type of proof that would have been good enough to hang people in England not all that long ago.

Mary Armour

Another very well-known and respected Scottish medium, Mary Armour, from Millport, has sat in many physical circles over a thirty year period, including that of the aforementioned Rita Goold, and she is willing to share some of these experiences with you and me within this book. For this I am grateful.

I have to stress that there is no substitute for personal experience in any avenue of paranormal inquiry, but maybe we can just glean the flavour of the experiences if we imagine ourselves actually being there and seeing them for ourselves.

Her first account is of a materialisation séance held in Berkley Street Spiritualist Church in Glasgow; the medium was Colin Fry. This church must hold about 60 people. Accompanying Mary that night was a medical doctor who was interested in these matters. It was stated by the medium beforehand that permission might be given, during the séance, for the doctor to take the pulse of a materialised figure.

Colin began the evening, as per usual, in a cabinet. At one point during the séance a personality by the name of Dolly, materialised. Dolly seemingly made a regular appearance at these events and often acted as a kind of master of ceremonies, or should I say mistress of ceremonies as Dolly claims to have been a drag queen. At a particular time during the materialisation, permission was given for the doctor to take Dolly's pulse and also the pulse of the medium. The doctor noted immediately that the hands of Dolly were considerably bigger than the hands of the medium and the pulses were quite different both in frequency and rhythm.

So with reference to the last two accounts, from different witnesses, we have a situation where fingerprints and a pulse have been recorded from two separate materialised figures. I find this very interesting.

Vignettes

Mary sat in circle with the physical medium, Stewart Alexander for many years and it was during one of these sessions that Mary's mother, Flossie, first appeared. When she was alive she vehemently expressed the opinion that she thought that survival was a lot of nonsense. As far as the family were concerned Flossie was also known to be quite a carnaptious[2] woman. When she made contact with Mary at this séance Mary said to her, 'Do you believe in this now?' The slow and caustic reply was received, 'Well....I don't have much option, do I.'

Mary 1 - Mother 0, I believe?

Another experience that Mary had in Stewart's physical circle was when a Dr Barnett materialised and came out of the cabinet; he approached Mary holding a large green illuminated, almost phosphorescent, ball in his hands. On another occasion Dr Barnett, who was a fairly old gentleman, approached her in the circle, but not illuminated this time, and gave her hands-on healing. Mary says that she could feel the long, aged, bony fingers as they went down her back.

---

[2] Author's note for non Scots; carnaptious means bad tempered and often disagreeable.

Up to that point Mary had been quite unwell and she declares that the 'energy' that came from that healing was just amazing and from that point she regained her normal health.

Mary's husband Joe often accompanied her to various séances and through the years he has also had some wonderful experiences. In a different circle, where I do not have permission to name the medium, a voice said that John was coming to speak to Joe. Joe said 'Is that you Jack?', thinking that it was his father, but the voice said, 'No, it's your brother John'. Now, his brother John was a very big man. What happened then was that in front of Joe there materialised a human arm, an illuminated lower arm which held its hand out in the position of a handshake. Joe took the hand and shook it and sure enough it was a very large hand which was in keeping with the size of his brother. He ran his other hand up the forearm to about the elbow – beyond that point there was nothing...empty space...no upper arm.

Mary has had Helen Duncan come to her through several mediums. She says that Helen has a code when approaching her and that code is always used before Helen makes herself known. Mary gives us all the advice and a warning that people are not always who they say they are when they come through; that is why every circle needs a strong, experienced, circle leader. Mary has Helen's voice on many, many, tapes, and I have heard some of these. When Helen comes to a sitter, in a circle sitting for automatic writing, the pencil is always moved to the medium's left hand. A pencil is normally always placed at the right hand of the medium, awaiting a communicator. You will gather from this that Helen Duncan was left handed.

Mary tells me that when the police raided a building where Helen Duncan was holding a séance, a woman police constable was running about trying to find the dog that was there when they barged in. Little did she know that it was a dog that had materialised within the circle! Funnily enough the policewoman never found it.

Jim Sherlock

Along with the phenomenon of actual materialisation it may be of interest to look at other events that can take place within a physical séance. The following accounts are by a gentleman called Jim Sherlock.

'These are some of my experiences with Physical mediumship:-

I've always known of the spirit world as I have seen & communicated with spirits both as a child and as an adult, so the next step seemed natural – to try and bring spirits through for others, especially the non-believers. I had read many books relating to great physical mediums, Alex Harris , John Sloan, Helen Duncan, etc. I wanted to see the modern mediums but as Stewart Alexander had stopped public displays I had to seek out others. Within a year I had seen those which I think are the top ones in the world – Kai Muegge, (Germany),Tom & Kevin (France), David Thompson (Australia), Bill Meadows, Warren Caylor and young Scott Milligan, all from England. As I was sitting for materialisation development myself, I wanted to see the differences in the methodology of the top ones and how they worked to bring through the deceased, since there were and are no teachers for this type of work except spirit.

My first experience with Kai Muegge was as follows. Kai did his holotropic breathing to induce his deep trance state and after what seemed like about ten minutes, his control, Hans Bender, came through.

I had previous experience in other physical medium demonstrations and had always felt an energy drain from my head with the energy going towards the medium, but this was nothing compared with the way I felt while sitting with Kai. At some stages I thought my head would blow up. When the energy drain was at its worst a voice said, "Are you all right Jim?" which at the same time relieved the draining, but how did this spirit know my head was becoming so sore? Then came the spirit lights, very bright lights about an inch in diameter going up like a roman candle, very bright, very clear. After another few minutes I saw my mother (who passed on four years previously) in the séance room. I whispered to my partner Mari, who sat on my right, that I had just seen my mother, just as Hans Bender said, 'We have a mother here looking for her son.' He then gave a very personal message to me from my mother. Hans explained that my mother could not speak because of her high emotions. Obviously the emotions in the room were very high and then when my mother came over to me and put her head on my shoulder and stroked my face & hair the tears flowed (tears of joy), then still with her head on my shoulder, she leaned over and stroked Mari's hair. A German lady, Bridgette who sat on my left, also felt my mother when her head was on my shoulder. Prof Hans Bender then said that my mother gives me a symbol of a thistle (a wild Scottish flower) which was significant as we had just called our private circle *The Thistles of Scotland* the day before. My mother was seen by all and appeared to be self-illuminating. Then my mother withdrew back into the cabinet. Kai then, in red light, demonstrated ectoplasm exuding from his mouth and as we watched, Hans Bender took control of Kai's hands and he started to rip the ectoplasm apart, showing pieces of the candyfloss like substance. We could see that something had formed in the ectoplasm and then an apport appeared; a crystal fell out and was given to me. Hans Bender said, 'This is a gift from your mother which will help in your development to become a physical medium.' A treasure I value highly.'

At a David Thompson demonstration.

'We were given a quick lecture on do's & don'ts in the séance room; I was picked as an independent checker, along with another lady. I searched David thoroughly as well as the cabinet and examined the cable ties on his legs and wrists and also the gag on his mouth. The séance started with an opening prayer and after about three upbeat songs William materialized. (David's control) He spoke to a few of us individually. He put his hand on my head and made a joke about some men's hands being bigger than others, (he did have very large hands) and after having a conversation with this man I could feel a strong loving power from this gentleman. Next to come through was Timmy, (Timothy Booth) the child spirit in charge of exuding the ectoplasm from David and raising the energies of the sitters. Trumpet phenomena began which were very fast and clear. Two trumpets moved very quickly around the room and very close to our faces, within millimetres. A figure then materialised for one of the sitters whom she recognised as her father. Emotions were running high now but then from the ectoplasmic voice box a father shouted the name of his son, who was by now an elderly man in his 80s. The old gentleman didn't hear at first and the spirit repeated his name shouting "Are you deaf?" to which the old man replied, 'Yes I am a bit'; this sitter was given very good evidence that subsequently proved to be correct, after he checked the information with his own son at a later date.'

Tom & Kevin

'I have been to France a few times to witness Tom & Kevin demonstrate physical mediumship and to talk with their spirit control, John Campbell Sloan. (The same man who, when alive, demonstrated physical mediumship to Arthur Findlay.) On my second visit to France I was also lucky enough to have the pleasure of seeing Mr Bill Meadows demonstrate. He was there with his circle linking up with Tom & Kevin's own circle; a first, I think, in bringing two physical circles together. At one point during this event the two mediums were levitated many feet up in the air on two heavy chairs at each side of the séance room. In red light conditions later we also all shook the hand of a spirit from the Meadows circle, saw the hairs on the back of this hand and felt the warmth of the flesh even although this person had been dead for many years.'

Warren Caylor

'Warren's spirit team was the most powerful I had come across yet. Warren was securely tied with cable ties, bound and gagged and a hood placed over his head, a procedure which I thought rather extreme but Warren was happy with it. The lights were put out and there were only a few tab lights around and a very bright light coming from a plaque on the floor near to my foot. I was asked to turn the plaque over when the séance was ready to begin.

We opened in prayer and after some preliminaries Winston Churchill came through to explain the workings behind the scenes in spirit and told us about a spirit light show that we were about to witness. It started with very loud bangs from the cabinet followed by a sound like fingers tapping all around the room, from one side of the cabinet, going right around the room to the other side of the cabinet. Then two trumpets rose to about head level and flew around the half of the room nearest the cabinet, right in front of me. Lights started to shine out of the trumpets, like torch beams shining on walls, faces, clothes, the floor and then the lights got brighter like lighthouse beams and the lights were now shining from the small end of the trumpets. Then, like a scene from close encounters, the lights started flashing on and off to the beat of a piece from *The Nutcracker*; very bright, very fast, and always in time with the music, it was amazing.

The circle control then asked us to turn over the plaque and he would show his hand on it, but the plaque was too bright. He then asked me to put it under the curtain and he would dull it down, which he did, which in itself was fantastic; he then showed his hands on the plaque, which everyone saw. After that Warren's clothes were thrown out from the cabinet onto our laps. The control, Yellow Feather, then asked if we wanted to see ectoplasm; no need to tell you the answer from us.

Yellow Feather then asked to control the red light. On the count of three he put on the red light, then on another count to three it was turned off again. Spirit controlled the curtain – they opened it about ten inches as we counted aloud – light on – but only a few of us saw the ectoplasm coming out of Warren's nostrils so Yellow Feather said he would do it again and opened the curtain wider. It was a fantastic cheese-clothy looking ectoplasm that was coming out of Warren's nostrils, going up over the curtain rail and formed into a perfect little hand with the index finger pointing out. That little formed hand, which looked perfect, was awesome and I will never forget it for the rest of my life. There was more to come, Winston Churchill said they would try and give Silvia (our host) a nice surprise for her birthday – they would dematerialise Warren and then bring Silvia into the cabinet to check. Warren was duly dematerialised and Silvia checked that he wasn't in the cabinet and then the chair was raised into the air. It was a wonderful evening and a wonderful demonstration from Warren, whom I had never met before.'

Jim's understanding of ectoplasm is from the Greek ektos, meaning "outside", and plasma, meaning "something formed or moulded." The word was first used or coined (invented) by Charles Richet to describe spiritual energy extruded (pulled out) of a physical or materialisation medium. To make it easier, try to imagine a jelly-like substance that can be moulded and manipulated.

So, what choice of the aforementioned four possibilities do you think best fits all of these examples of materialisation and other phenomena? Human source, external source, fraud, or delusion?

If it is all delusion then an awful lot of people have been fooled, and I do not think this for a minute. Everyone must examine each case on its own merits and draw your own conclusions, but make sure that your conclusions fit the actual facts.

The following quote may be useful here.

Sit down before fact as a little child, be prepared to give up every preconceived notion, follow humbly wherever and to whatever abysses nature leads, or you shall learn nothing.

—THOMAS HENRY HUXLEY

Chapter 3

DROP-IN COMMUNICATORS

I think that the evidence obtained from the examination of the phenomenon of the drop-in communicator is extremely important, as it throws up a great number of cogs into the wheel of hardened sceptics. I have referred to this phenomenon in my last book, but I would like to enlarge on this now as I feel that the type of information given in this type of situation is very difficult to 'explain away' or account for through any rational means that we have at our fingertips. If anyone wants to call it ESP or telepathy it must be ESP or telepathy between the medium and an active discarnate intelligence, as no one else in the room has knowledge of, or information about, the 'drop-in'. If it is the downloading of a file from some sort of cosmic consciousness, why would a file have the impetus to butt in and make the contents of that file known to the sitters? There has to have been a motivating factor on the part of the drop-in as the sitters had no relationship to, or indeed any interest in, that deceased person.

To recap, a drop-in communicator is a person of unknown identity to anyone in the room, including the medium, who makes himself or herself known at a séance, where people are gathered together for the purpose of contacting deceased personalities, be they friends, family, Elvis or whoever. Most séances are set up for either 'spiritual enlightenment' through the teachings of the people who purport to come through on a regular basis, or to keep in touch with the friends and relatives of those sitting in the séance circle.

As far as I am aware, Dr Alan Gauld is actually the person who has done the most research on this phenomenon and I, for one, am most grateful to him. I think that it is very important that people should know of these matters and take them seriously.

Dr Gauld was given transcripts of séances that were held many years previous to his inquiries. As far as I am aware he actually inherited them. I am not sure if he originally actually wanted them. However, on perusal of these transcripts, he noted that quite a few people had 'come through' who were unknown to anyone within that circle.

The actual sitters in that circle at the time did not bother to check up on these drop-ins as they had no real interest in them, and in fact probably thought of them as a bit of a nuisance, but Alan was curious to find out if these people had ever actually existed.

The cases studied by Dr Gauld occurred during a series of sittings by a small group of people who met at the home of a Mr Smith (*pseudonym*). The experiments, using a Ouija board, began in 1937; sessions were also held during the Second World War from 1942 - 1945 continuing thereafter until 1954. (Yes! I know that I never advocate the use of a Ouija board, but that is how they did it.) Other sessions were held in later years. The majority of the sittings, with dates, were recorded in writing by Mr Smith in old exercise books or memo pads. It was hard work to do so as the answers to questions were spelled out immediately the question was asked. Occasionally over the years a sitter would drop out and a newcomer would be allowed to join the circle. The circle seemed to have a control/guide of sorts called 'Peter' who nearly always acted like an intermediary for other ostensible deceased communicators. 'Peter' took a somewhat proprietary attitude to 'his' circle.

In the records of the 470 sittings that remained from this circle, 240 alleged communicators manifested. Most claimed to be deceased relatives or friends of the sitters but in addition there were 37 unknown communicators. In Dr Gauld's published study he gives the results of his inquiries about those who had provided sufficient details about themselves for attempts to be made to ascertain if they *had ever* existed and if the details provided by them could be verified.

In his study Dr Gauld points out that not only did the sitters never seek publicity or money, but also they did not undertake serious investigations into the 'drop-in' communicators; after all, although they were invariably polite to these communicators they were looked upon as intruding strangers. Dr Gauld, himself, made his investigations thirteen to twenty-eight years after the information had been communicated. The following cases are outlines of just two of them: Gustav Adolf Biedermann, who appeared as a 'drop-in' on a number of occasions in January and February, 1943 and Harry Stockbridge, who appeared eleven times between July 3rd, 1950 and July 14th, 1952. Both were introduced to the circle members by the circle's control 'Peter', who, as already pointed out, acted as a sort of 'master of ceremonies' every week. It is of interest to note that the first time Biedermann came through he actually refused to give his name.

The Biedermann Case.

This occurred during the Second World War. In the first sittings at which Biedermann came through he was thoroughly obnoxious, rude, sarcastic, arrogant, and openly contemptuous of women and indeed of most of humanity, although he expressed his fervent admiration for Adolf Hitler. He was also openly scornful of the attempts made by members of the circle to be friendly and to help him understand his situation.

As time passed during these sessions, he did eventually give his name and inadvertently boastfully provided relevant information regarding his career and occupations, the places he worked, his address in London, the age at which he died, even his views on religion - he claimed to be a rationalist who scorned all forms of religion. (I wonder where he thought he was speaking from?)

As time went by he became a lot quieter about the great Hitler, as it was becoming clear that things were not particularly going his way, and by the end of his last visit he seemed to have mellowed and become sincerely grateful for the patient friendship shown to him by the circle. He apologised to them and hoped that he would continue to make progress in his present 'situation.'

Having studied the information that Biedermann had revealed, in 1964 Dr Gauld began an attempt to see whether anyone fitting the Biedermann data and psychological profile could be found. His exhaustive investigation was successful. There *had* been a man of that name and almost every statement given by him was found to be correct. The statement that he had known Hitler was not followed up, since it was obvious that he had doubtless made it to offend the sitters. Sir Cyril Burt, who assisted Gauld in his inquiries regarding Biedermann, wrote:

He had the blunt, arrogant, obstinate and aggressive manner of the typical Prussian Junker. Hence he was not very well liked; but, when one got past the outer facade, he turned out to be quite a pleasant companion. He was, like your communicator, fond of 'denouncing' things - and I am pretty sure that one of them would have been religion.

As part of his investigation Dr Gauld questioned the members of the circle, all but one of whom were still alive, and concluded that it was in the highest degree unlikely that any of them had had any contact with or any detailed information about Biedermann. Dr Gauld also points out that the items of information could have been collated in casual reading only from at least four of the public sources of information about Biedermann. Only in his will and/or death certificate could all the items have been found. Dr Gauld, in his paper, gives a cogent argument against the likelihood of deliberate fraud.

It is interesting to note that in this case, as with some other phenomena, a discarnate personality seemed to know about changing events on Earth since their demise. In this case Biedermann became quieter and quieter about Hitler as he must have realised that his hero wasn't doing so well. This thought alone is very interesting and throws up even more questions.

The Harry Stockbridge Case.

This second example of Harry Stockbridge was again introduced by 'Peter', who said that this gentleman wanted to work with the circle. In the ten or so sittings where he manifested, he showed that he was in temperament quite unlike Biedermann; he was a very lively communicator and indulged in a good bit of, as we might say in Scotland, banter. Nevertheless, he gave items of information about himself and his life that, like pieces of a jigsaw puzzle, when put together made a coherent picture.

Stockbridge claimed to be a soldier from the First World War, killed on July 14th, 1916. He mentioned the Tyneside Scottish and that he had been in rank Second Loot and attached to the Northumberland Fusiliers. In a further sitting he said that he, 'Hung out in Leicester, Leicester holds a record. I would laugh if doubted when you confirm my existence.'

Mr Smith's wife was, according to Dr Gauld, probably the medium in the circle. Some months after the sitting in which Leicester was mentioned, Mr Smith woke up one morning convinced that he knew the name of the street in Leicester in which Stockbridge was born. He mentioned this to Mrs Smith. Without being told, she replied 'Powis'. When Harry Stockbridge next appeared on July 14th, 1952, Mrs Smith asked him about Powis Street. Stockbridge replied, 'I knew it well. My association took my memory there.'

He described himself as being tall, dark and thin with dark brown eyes. In passing, it is not without interest that the dates of three of the drop-in's appearances out of eleven, namely 3rd, 10th and 14th of July, are dates in the month in which he died, the 14th of July 1952 in fact being the thirty-sixth anniversary of his death.

Dr Gauld's exhaustive and diligent search, began in 1965, and was markedly productive. A Second Lieutenant H. Stockbridge of the North-umberland Fusiliers appears in the War Office official list *Officers died in the Great War of 1914 - 1919*. He is stated to have been killed on July 19th, 1916, not 14th July, 1916, as claimed by the communicator. Stock-bridge's death certificate, however, gives his date of death as 14th July, 1916. In order to clarify this discrepancy, Gauld wrote to the Army Records Centre and asked which date appeared in the officer's file. He received the reply: 'I am to refer to your letter DAG/JHW dated 15th November 1966 and to inform you that according to the records held, 2nd Lieutenant Stockbridge was killed in action on 14th July 1916.'

So the information from the drop-in was *correct* and the official published list was wrong!

Stockbridge's birth certificate gives his year and place of birth as 1896 and Leicester. Dr Gauld was also informed that this also appeared in Joseph Keating's *Tyneside Irish Brigade* [London, 1917] but was un-able to discover any regimental history in which Stockbridge's name appeared. Keating records Stockbridge as an officer in one of the Ty-neside Irish Battalions of the Northumberland Fusiliers. Nevertheless Gauld was led to understand that records contained in the War Of-fice Library show that at the time he died, Stockbridge was attached to a Tyneside Scottish Battalion of the Northumberland Fusiliers. (As stated by the drop-in communicator.)

Indeed the other claim by the 'drop-in', *'Leicester holds a record'* was soundly vindicated. There is in that city a Powis Street a few hundred yards from the house in which Stockbridge was born.

Further researches by Dr Gauld included success in contacting two of Stockbridge's brothers. Their description of his appearance, and a photograph of him, preserved in the archives of his old school, supported the drop-in's description that was given – tall, dark, thin, large brown eyes. Again, Gauld was forced to the conclusion that, like the Biedermann case, fraud or coincidence could not account for the Stockbridge case. The medium and sitters in the circle did not know anything about Stockbridge, far less had heard of him.

We are reminded of the quotes:-

I didn't say it was possible, I just said that it happened

—SIR WILLIAM CROOKES

Minds are like parachutes.
They only function when they are open.

—LORD THOMAS DEWAR

Concerning the phenomenon of drop-in communicators and other phenomena such as apparitions, materialisation, authentic poltergeist cases with a discarnate influence and spiritual healing, there appears to be an involvement with a deceased personality, or personalities. In these cases the people appear to have chosen, for various reasons, to 'return' from their appointed place to make themselves known to people still alive, and display that there are indeed *things they can do when they are dead.*

I would now like to consider the plight of people who have, for one reason or another, maybe not quite made it over to the 'other side' properly in the first place.

Chapter 4

EARTHBOUNDS

The idea of survival of human personality after death is a common thread in most religions. Psychical researchers look for evidence which may enhance or negate this belief. The Christian Churches Fellowship for Spiritual and Psychic studies in the UK has a motto; *to belief add knowledge.* This seems very sensible to me.

Through experience, it would appear to me that when some people die they do not easily move on to 'wherever' they should go, but appear to be stuck. It would seem that they can be stuck by choice, ignorance of the fact that they are actually dead or simply that they don't know how to move on. So what can we, on Earth, do to try to help this situation?

The Church of England have several diocese of 'healing' or 'deliverance' which I believe used to be called healing and exorcism. Like myself, many ministers do not actually approve of, or like, the word exorcism, due to its connotations, but some people will still insist on using it. When ministers of this Church call on families experiencing some kind of disturbance they ask themselves questions such as, 'Does this house, or someone in it, need healing?' Whether it is poltergeist activity, sightings of apparitions or any other phenomenon that has been reported, they call it deliverance ministry. There are 43 geographical diocese in the Church of England and many of them have their own 'Deliverance' team. One of the issues that they deal with is that of earthbound personalities.

The Revd. Canon Michael Perry edited a book called *Deliverance*, subtitled 'Psychic disturbances and occult involvement', which contains advice on this type of work in relation to the Church of England and the Church of Wales. This book gives guidance and structure to their ministers and priests in assessing incidents and how to deal with them, such as those in the earthbound category.

The best way to describe this category is to give some examples.

Earthbound Airmen

In the north of England there was a particular area of land used as an RAF station during the Second World War. Some years after the war, the land was taken over by a very large construction firm, the type of company that trains people in the operation of very large heavy machinery. So no "airy fairy" personalities were involved in the following events.

The structure of one of the old hangers had been kept and made into squash courts for the company's staff. This proved to be very popular for a while until the owners noticed that there was a tail-off and hardly anyone was using the courts at all. When subtle inquiries were made people very sheepishly admitted that they didn't like playing there as they felt as if someone was watching them, and it gave them a kind of creepy feeling. It was becoming so marked that the owners quietly asked a Church of England minister to have a look at the situation. It so happened that this minister's wife was mediumistic. When she accompanied him to the site she said that there was definitely 'something' there and that they should return and try to communicate with whatever it was. Subsequently they returned with a tape recorder and another two witnesses. Not only was the minister's wife naturally mediumistic but she was also a trance medium. This meant that she could alter her consciousness and take herself 'out' of the situation and allow any deceased person to talk through her. I have a tape recording of the whole proceedings.

Once the medium was in trance, the minister asked the usual question, 'Is there anyone there who wishes to communicate?' For anyone who does not know what trance mediumship is, it means that any reply would come through the physical body of the medium. Remember that the medium was a woman. After a short wait the following occurred.

Reply (R) A man's very weak and shivery voice replied save us; help us! help us!

Minister (M) 'How can we help you?'

R. Can you hear me?

M. Yes, I can hear you, tell us what happened... (more shivering is heard)... tell us what happened.

R. Plane... Fire... (slow response in a very faint voice)

M. The plane went on fire and crashed?....... Where?'

R. Near here—near a church (all very slow, faint and shivery), then the voice said, 'Dusty Miller' (very faint)

M. Is it a man?

R. The voice continued... 'Pat Sullivan... Gerry Arnold' (all names were delivered slowly in a very quiet, shivering, almost painful voice)

M. Cherry Arnold? Another witness said no, Gerry Arnold.

R. Help us... help us!

M. What can we do? hum... pause,... then in a strong positive voice he said, 'You know that you have left the earth behind? In the plane you died. (Pause). Do you know that?'

R. Help!

M. You are to look up, because you are keeping yourselves down, you are to look up. Look up for help! There is help there, when you see some coming go towards them. You don't belong here anymore, do you understand that? – short silence.

R. There is a light (still shivering)

M. The light...is it a good light...a white light?

R .....Yes (still shivering)

M *Pull* yourselves towards that light, go towards it...but you are afraid of going aren't you? Well don't be afraid you'll find help there... but you're cold. Were you in water... were your feet in water?

R. Yes (quiet and shivering)

M. Look up!... don't be afraid... let go of the Earth,... ask for help... you don't belong here. But you're holding yourselves down. Tell Dusty, Gerry, Pat... will you do that? God bless you.

This is followed by moments of silence punctuated by a strange sound which is really hard to describe other than like a long electrical discharge, a kind of a slow whooshing noise which lasted about 5 seconds.

Then a completely different male voice came through the medium – solid, deep, vibrant and I would proffer very spiritual. The type of voice that makes the hairs stand up on the back of your neck.

Voice. (V) My children, I give thanks for the help which you have given my medium and those on this side of life.

M. Are they all right now?

V. At this time they are now being helped and it has been almost thirty years since this help has been sought for and at last they can now be happy. You will hear no more of disturbances and should you hear any such stories then you will realise that this is but the person's own mind. I give thanks for all the help that you have given. Bless you.

This whole intervention took approximately 10 minutes.

After subsequent enquiries, it was found that in fact three young airmen had died around that area near the end of World War Two. Their names were indeed, Dusty Miller, Gerry Arnold and Pat Sullivan.

Reading this account does not impart the emotion that this interview holds – it is electric. However, as I always say, *the proof of the pudding is in the eating* and after that 'clearance' the employees of the construction firm gradually came back to the squash courts and no further experiences were reported. Remember that the employees were not told of the minister's interface and therefore psychological factors did not come into play in this instance.

Two particular phrases jumped out at me upon reflection of this dialogue. One was, 'Is it a good light?' and after asking if the airmen were now all right the reply was, 'At this time they are now being helped...' We can all draw our own conclusions about these phrases, but somehow they feel particularly 'correct' to me.

The Exorcist.

The following account was written by Archie Roy and given to me for use in this book.

'In the course of his ministry as a priest in the Church of England my friend Tony Duncan became completely convinced of the occurrence of a wide variety of paranormal phenomena. After Army service, he entered the Church and his first charge was in a small English town, almost a village. He and his family – his wife and three sons – took up residence in the spacious vicarage. In front of it there was the village green and on the other side of the village green was the church. The vicarage was so big that each of his sons had his own bedroom, the eldest, David, being installed upstairs in a large room, complete with a small dressing room, the bedroom window opening onto a view of the village green and the church on the other side of the green. At first everyone in the family seemed very happy with their lot but Tony began to notice that his eldest son seemed uncharacteristically subdued and morose.

Tony had a talk with him. The boy told him that although naturally he was pleased to have his own bedroom, he was unhappy because of the man he sometimes saw standing at the window and looking outside. Apart from the fact that the man would appear and stand there for some time before vanishing, he seemed to bring with him feelings of unhappiness and failure.

Although Tony took it upon himself to stay at intervals in the bedroom, he himself did not experience anything of the sort his son had. Two further events however caused the vicar to adopt a certain course of action. A few weeks after his son told him about the man, a family friend came to stay with them. The friend had a certain reputation of being a sensitive and on the spur of the moment, without telling his friend anything about the man in the bedroom, Tony gave him a tour of the vicarage. In David's bedroom, the friend hesitated. He finally said, "You have an earthbound in here...an old man. He means no harm."

The second event happened soon afterwards. David happened to be in the church vestry a few days later. It was the first time he had been in that room. He looked round the walls on which were photographs of some of the previous vicars. "Dad," he exclaimed, pointing to one of the photographs, "That's the man who appears in my bedroom."

Tony began to make cautious and diplomatic enquiries among his more elderly parishioners and a picture began to form. The old vicar had, during the last years of his incumbency, become convinced that he had let the parish down by his uninspired preaching as the number of worshippers in his church had significantly fallen during those last years and he had, in a sense, retreated within himself. Now something of him still seemed to be present in David's bedroom and perhaps in some way was still conscious of looking out of the bedroom window, across the village green to the church he believed he had failed.

Tony gathered his family about him and told them what he had found out about George Carstairs (*pseudonym*). He ended by saying, "Now look here people, it appears that in some way old George is stuck here. We're going to hold a service in David's bedroom, a service of release. We're going to help George to move on."

In his training to be a priest Tony had of course read of rescue missions, services of deliverance and release but had never before utilised any of the procedures. Now he read them up again; he also prepared by prayerfully invoking heavenly aid. The day arrived for the service and his family gathered in David's bedroom. Tony told me that they were determined through love to help the old vicar to break free from his earthbound state, realise that there were others on the other side waiting to help him and that he had in no way separated himself from the love of God.

The service proceeded and to Tony it was apparent that his family was with him in his efforts. And then it happened. While he prayed and, naming Mr Carstairs, urged him to move towards the light where there were people waiting to help him, the atmosphere suddenly lifted as if the sun had come out from behind a cloud and Tony himself saw, standing in the entrance between the bedroom and little dressing room, the figure of the vicar. The old man smiled at him, sending a message of thanks so clearly to Tony and his family that Tony knew immediately that they had been successful. In fact the figure of the old vicar was never seen again and the room's gloomy atmosphere was completely dispersed.

It was a turning point in Tony's ministry. Later in his career he was appointed chief exorcist in an English diocese. He was called in to all kinds of cases where ostensible paranormal events were taking place. He became familiar with a wide variety of cases and was able to help many of the families involved. He did say however that there was a rare form of case that was difficult if not impossible to deal with in a satisfactory way. On one such occasion he was called out to a family who had recently moved into an old house. Before they did so they had been happy and contented, functional and loving, concerned for each other. Within a few months of the move they had become a totally dysfunctional family, irritating each other, nagging each other, seemingly almost obsessed at finding fault and picking quarrels. They were in an extremely miserable state. Somehow they knew themselves that there was something dreadfully wrong with their present behaviour. It was almost as if they were continually being influenced in some malignant fashion by some unseen Iago. Tony, after a great deal of talk with the family members and an investigation into the house's history, had to take seriously the theory that the house still contained an active personality of some kind who took a perverse pleasure in causing the maximum amount of pain and misery it could in anyone living there. He finally had to advise the family to sell the house. He really would have liked to advise the family to burn the house but of course he could not go as far as that.

Unlike old George Carstairs, the vicar who thought he had failed his parishioners and whose apparition appeared but obviously had no intention of causing trouble, there might in some situations be an active, interfering, mischievous earthbound entity delighting in causing trouble with the living. For most people that is a hard idea to accept. Many would probably class it as mediaeval superstition. But if in some way human personality survives bodily death, we certainly cannot assume that a nasty person is automatically transformed by death into a much more benign, caring person any more than we would suppose a kind, loving, unselfish person is transformed by death into a villain. Nor can we avoid the possibility that some who die might linger on in a totally confused state, close to living human beings, and are able on occasion to trigger physical phenomena whose unpredictable and nonsensical nature is at least as alarming as the phenomena themselves.'

We have now looked at two completely different cases. The trapped airmen whose plane crashed near that building site who, to all intents and purposes, did not appear to know that they were dead, or perhaps they were, just as the minister said, afraid to move on or perhaps they did not know *how* to move on. It was interesting that the first thing they said, once they could speak through the medium, was 'Save us, help us.'

As I said, the recording of this 'clearance' is very atmospheric, such a lot of emotion. I wish that you could all hear it. How unlike the old minister who was so sad and who felt that he had let his Parish down and yet, he too was also unable to go forward without assistance.

The more that I look into these matters the more I realise how important our thoughts, intentions, motivation and expectations are. In fact I would go as far as to say that without emotion and intention none of these phenomena or their resolutions could occur.

I know that I am putting myself on the line by saying this but I believe in the following quotation by Erwin Schrodinger, and so did Professor Archie Roy.

'I can see no other escape from this dilemma... that some of us should venture to embark on a synthesis of facts and theories, albeit with second-hand and incomplete knowledge of some of them and at the risk of making fools of ourselves.'

Chapter 5

POLTERGEIST ACTIVITY, ET AL

The word poltergeist is often misused. Poltergeist is not so much a thing or a person but a method of behaviour and that is why I speak about poltergeist activity, which often displays behaviour similar to that of a spoiled child who cannot get its own way or get a point across. The resulting phenomena can sometimes appear to be destructive or frightening. It appears that some activity can be caused by a sort of psychic remnant from the past. However, there are many more common benign forms of poltergeist activity, appearing to be from a deceased person, which seem to be 'in the moment' and have the motivation of letting someone know that the person who has passed is 'ok'. Sometimes poltergeist activity is accompanied by apparitional phenomena, but certainly not always.

Oh! There you are!

About four years ago I was asked to visit a family in Ayrshire as their small boy was complaining about the 'girl' in his room.

I took another colleague with me and we videotaped interviews.

Both parents had good jobs and the father worked different shift patterns. They had three children, an older girl, the boy and a baby girl about a year old. They were a very nice family with a positive attitude to life. The boy was just under five years of age and was quite a vocal character. When he was alone in his room the mother would often hear him speaking to someone. When she asked whom he was talking to he simply said, 'the girl.' She paid little attention to this, thinking that it was his imagination. However as time went by he began to complain to his mum that the girl was keeping him awake at night by talking to him and he didn't like her anyway as she had 'bleedy' hands. This was becoming a real problem, so she asked him about the girl. He said that she was bigger than him and she wore a white dress down to 'there' (beneath the knees a couple of inches), white socks and black shiny shoes. She had a white face, longish dark hair and when she held her hands up with the palms towards him they were very red... like 'bleedy'. The father didn't believe a word of this, but the mum knew that her son was genuinely upset.

Sometime later, when the father came home during the day after a shift, he put his keys on top of the mantelpiece in the lounge and something strange happened. He was the only person in the house. He went into the kitchen to put on the kettle or something like that and while he was there he heard a strange sound from the lounge. It was a metallic sound, like keys jingling. He was puzzled and went back into the lounge to witness the keys on top of the mantelpiece physically moving up and down on their own and making this loud jingling noise. He lifted the keys, told no one, and pretended that it had not happened.

Another day he was in the kitchen, again alone in the house, when he turned around to be met by the gaze of a girl standing in the doorway between him and the lounge. She was staring at him with a sad and blank expression, she looked about ten years old and she was wearing a white dress, white ankle socks and black shiny shoes.

He freaked out and the girl disappeared.

It was at this point that the mother called me. A colleague and I visited the house and interviewed the mum, the older sister and to a much lesser extent the boy. I say this because the child kept momentarily flitting in and out of the room during the interviews where I could assess that he was not a shrinking violet. Latterly as he danced past me I said to him, 'Tell me about this girl that comes to your room. How tall is she?' He lifted an arm up as high as he could while standing on his tip-toes and said 'this tall.' As he was escaping out of the door I said, 'Do you know what her name is?' Quick as a flash he said 'Daphne' and then he was gone.

We made another appointment to interview the father.

In between our visits the family had asked an old neighbour if anything unusual had ever happened in this house. She thought that there had been a fire in that block many years ago and that a little girl had died.

The father had yet another shock to come. One day, just before our second visit, he was having a shower in the bathroom, which is upstairs. He drew back the shower curtain to exit the shower to be met by the fixed gaze of the little girl standing in the doorway of the bathroom. The description was as before, sad and pale, appearing to be looking straight at him.

I don't think that I need to describe his reaction.

Now he believed his son.

The father confirmed all of the events described and was really very shaken up.

We brought a medium with us on a subsequent visit, but sad to say we never really got to the bottom of this one and I have heard nothing since. Who knows, maybe it will resurface again in the future.

The Old Chapel House Case

This is a case which is "a game of two halves"; (as someone famously said about football). The initial investigation was carried out by Archie Roy, and I came into the picture later on.

It was the housing officer of the smallish town in which the chapel house case occurred who brought the case to Archie's attention. She, somewhat cautiously, contacted him in his office at Glasgow University. After he reassured her that he was listening and taking her seriously she told of a young couple who had moved into a nearby chapel house, occupying the upper storey. The two flats shared a main door into the lobby then split into upper and lower flats.

Various inexplicable and alarming events had so terrified them that they had fled to the council house of the young man's parents. They were living there now in crowded conditions and refused to go back to the rather beautiful chapel house. The housing officer's description of the happenings and the state of mind of the young couple persuaded Professor Roy to have a meeting with them. On the 21st November 1984 he drove to a little town between Glasgow and Edinburgh with a colleague, Ron Cassidy. The meeting took place in the parents' house. Present were Jenny and Peter Andrews (the young couple), Peter's brother, Kevin, Peter's parents, Mr and Mrs Andrews, Ron Cassidy and Prof Roy. The session was tape-recorded, as is the advised protocol of an investigation, so that the account could be studied at a later date.

Peter told of events that had started on the previous Tuesday night, roughly about 3am. Quote. "Jenny was sleeping – I heard funny noises coming from down the stair – like doors banging. I thought that Jenny had forgotten to lock the doors so I picked up the keys of the house and went down the stairs to investigate the banging. The two doors appeared to be locked. I heard the banging coming from the lower flat. So I opened the door to get into the house below the stairs and all the doors appeared to be closed. Just then I turned around to make my way back up, up to our flat, when the figure, what I thought was a ghost, was standing in front of the doorway. It appeared to be big, wearing a dark cloak, just a vague dark shadow standing in the doorway. I got a fright, jumped back and asked it what it was doing there and I seemed to float in fresh air, just rise straight up into fresh air. And I asked it to put me down, twice I asked it to put me down and I seemed to go from vertical to lying flat on my back, floating in fresh air – and I was eye to eye with the ceiling then I was back on my feet again. I panicked, slammed the door shut, ran back upstairs to the house again, into bed. Tried to wake Jenny up – couldn't get any sign of life out of her at all. So I was thinking about if it was true, if what I seen was true or if it was not true, or what was happening. So I put my head down on the pillow to go back to sleep and every time I appeared to put my head on the pillow it seemed to be something was taking over me. Couldn't speak, I was going frozen but when I sat back up in my bed again it was o.k., everything was clear enough. So I lay back down again – same thing happened again, couldn't speak, frozen, couldn't move. Sat back up again quick, everything was o.k. Tried to waken up Jenny again to explain to her there was funny things going on in the house. I couldn't get any sense out of her so I smoked another cigarette, lay back down in bed again and this time I had no chance to get back up, I just froze. Couldn't speak, couldn't move – then the bedroom door opened about a foot to a foot and a half. I couldn't see nothing, couldn't sight nothing or nothing like that. Then I felt the bed going down. It was as though it was coming into bed with me; the blankets getting lifted, this thing getting into bed with me and I was trying to shout on Jenny but I was just speaking into fresh air, I couldn't open my mouth. And it seemed to poke me in the back and said, "You leave her alone, I'm warning you, you leave her alone" and those were the words it said to me. I came back to my senses again turned round quick and there was nobody in the room, but the bedroom door was still open. Tried to waken Jenny up for the third time, still couldn't get any sense out of her. She just seemed to be away in a world of her own like – just couldn't waken her up. And that's what occurred on the Tuesday night."

Up until the following Monday, the couple had visitors in the house at all times. The following is an account of events that occurred on that Monday evening.

"So we were in bed on Monday night, it was just much roughly about the same time, 2 o'clock – half past 2. I was in a sleep and Jenny woke me up, kicking me, shaking me, and shouting at me to wake up. And when I woke up I heard banging coming from the porch down the stair in the house; things getting flung about, things getting dragged, scuffed. Jenny was in a bit of a state of shock, crying, screaming. She was saying that she heard a song, a tape – something playing music, she heard the washing machine starting up and all this noise down the stair, like. And that was it; I says that's enough, like, we just can't take any more of this, so I phoned the police, 999, to get them to come and investigate. I was warned not to go anywhere near this noise, to stay in the same room. So when the police came to the house they checked the full bottom house, the grounds around about it and there was no appearance of any people there or anything like that. I mean there was just silence again; that was it. So we packed a few things and we left to come up here to stay at my mother's because we just weren't staying in the house any longer, like. There were too many weird things happening."

The investigators then asked if it was unusual that one or other had difficulty in wakening up the other. Peter replied, "Oh yes definitely. I mean that last Tuesday night when I was trying to waken up Jenny I was pushing her, pulling her, shouting at her – just couldn't get any sense out of her at all. She just kept saying, "I'm tired ...sleep."

Jenny agreed that she had equal difficulty in trying to waken Peter, and this was very unusual. When Peter was questioned further, Professor Roy (AER) asked again about the first series of events and asked him to recall which doors he had thought were banging. He replied the outside porch door. Professor Roy then replied, "The outside porch door; I see. And then you went downstairs and you saw this figure. Now let's come to the figure. Did you take it at all for granted that it was a real person?"

Reply: No.

AER. "And then you say that you went into a sequence of events whereby you seemed to be sort of raised and lowered?

Peter. "Just..., I floated straight up into the air. Twice I shouted it, 'Put me down you – put me down! And when I came to my senses I was back on the ground where I was at first, and the figure wasn't there any longer."

Mr Cassidy then asked if at any time he had a difficulty in breathing to which the answer was no.

AER. "Before it slips my mind; the downstairs place – is it a flat like this one in the sense that it is a furnished flat?"

Peter. "No – an empty house."

AER. "But is it a house?"

Peter. "Yes. It is all one house just one big house; just that the guy who owns the house, he's put a partition up and knocked the house into more or less two bits, an upstairs flat and a downstairs flat."

AER. "You said something on the phone about it being an old Chapel House?"

Peter. "The Manse."

Kevin. "The Roman Catholic priests in Cornton have lived there for many years. And the chapel, the first chapel is in the grounds of that house. They no longer required it when they built the new one and they moved away."

AER. "And so they sold it."

Peter. "Yes."

Peter. "There was one point I missed out."

AER. "Oh."

Peter. "After last Tuesday night, that thing happening to me, what happened on the Wednesday morning when I was speaking to Jenny about it, I mean that was after we'd been in the house a week, she had told me about an experience she had the second day we moved in. She was in the kitchen making the dinner and I had left to go and do a message. And she heard her name getting called out, 'Jenny... Jenny' – and she thought it was me in the house acting the goat."

AER. "I see, she didn't think it was you calling her in a natural voice. (Then to Jenny) You thought it was this man, sort of joking?"

Jenny. "Yes."

Peter. "So she says, 'If you want me come and get me in the kitchen'. Obviously no one appeared like so she left the kitchen, looked in the living room, couldn't see me, looked in the bedrooms for me, I wasn't there but her name was still getting called out, 'Jenny'... and she thought I was at the bottom of the stairs shouting up. So she thought, I'll give him a fright; I'll creep down the stairs, but when she got to the bottom of the stairs her name was still getting shouted but it was getting fainter as if it was going away in the distance. And it just clicked on her that it couldn't be me because if it had been me she would have heard the car. It just clicked on her that I was away out the place, like."

AER. "Now what was your reaction to this?"

Jenny. "I just put it out my mind because I wouldn't tell him about it, until after what happened to him because I thought he might have thought I was stupid."

Mr Cassidy. "I was just wondering about the first night that there were real problems when you went downstairs to see if the door was locked. After the events that you described, you heard a voice; how did it sound, was it gruff?"

Peter. "To be honest with you the voice I heard was the voice of my little brother."

Mr Cassidy. "Where was your young brother at the time?"

Peter. "He was up the top end of Cornton living with his girlfriend, lying in bed."

AER. "But it sounded like him?"

Peter. "Oh yes, I could have sworn it was his voice."

Mr Cassidy. "Did you see the door open on that occasion, did you say?"

Peter. "Yes I seen the door opening."

Mr Cassidy. "You were looking at the door as it opened?"

Peter. "Yes it was opening very slowly but I couldn't see nobody."

AER. "Now, you let me speak to the daughter of the owner of the house and she told us that she had once lived in the house. Now all the time that the upper flat was occupied, there would never be anyone downstairs because it is derelict, as you said, and she told us that her sister had stayed there for a short time, is that right?"

Peter. "Yes."

AER. "And did she experience anything out of the ordinary?"

Peter. "I honestly couldn't tell you."

AER. "So obviously we'll need to talk to her about these things."

Peter. "Yes."

AER. "You were referring to a time before you moved in when you found lights on in the place. What were the circumstances of this? About how long before you moved in did this occur?"

Peter. "It would be roughly about four months before we moved in. We got a phone call saying that we'd to go down. So the son of the place, he came up and picked us up and we went down to the place. We had been half thinking that there was a gang of youths down here smoking dope, you ken, and drinking. When we went in all the doors were still locked. We had to open the doors up and every light was on in the house, upstairs and downstairs."

Peter also recalled that when he and his brothers were decorating the chapel house, before he and Jenny moved into the upper flat, they had found themselves locked in. Their keys did not work and it was only when someone arrived with a spare set of keys that they were released. On trying their own keys again, they worked without difficulty.

The investigators were impressed overall with the sincerity of Peter and Jenny as they seemed genuinely bewildered and frightened by their experiences. They then went to visit the Chapel House. Peter unlocked the door and they entered. With the lights on the whole flat produced a pleasant impression, there was no sense of any cold feeling one can sometimes associate with reported paranormal events. It appeared to the investigators that only genuine fear would have made the young couple leave that spacious flat to live with Peter's parents in cramped conditions. Peter stated emphatically that there was no way he and Jenny were returning to that house and that was the end of it.

Professor Roy subsequently had an independent interview with Alice, the daughter of the owner of the house, as she had occupied the upper flat of the chapel house with her husband for the best part of a year. This was prior to Peter and Jenny's occupancy. As indicated before there was no one living downstairs because it was in a derelict condition. One night during their time in residence she woke up to hear noises, raps, bangs, crashes coming from downstairs. She woke her husband up and he too heard the sounds. Finally she suggested that he should go downstairs to see what was going on. He was reluctant to do so, so she got up out of bed, put on the light at the top of the stairs and went downstairs into the darkness accompanied by the big Alsatian dog that they sometimes used as a guard dog in the business they had previously owned. She found nothing in the hall at the foot of the stairs and the front door was closed and locked. She opened the door in the partition and with the dog entered the derelict flat. Everything was quiet, she could see nothing wrong so she turned to come out and found herself facing a tall black figure in what appeared to be a cloak and hood. She froze in a paralysis of fear. When asked what the dog did she replied, "It went mad with terror, fled upstairs and would not come down again."

AER. "And then what happened?

Alice. "Somehow I found myself upstairs, freezing cold, shivering...."

Alice and her husband moved to another house soon afterwards. On a personal note I am surprised that she was even speaking to him after his reluctance to investigate the alarming noises downstairs.

She told Professor Roy that she was certain that the guard dog's behaviour supported her conviction that the figure had not been "real", in the sense of not of this Earth. Out of curiosity she subsequently wrote to the old retired priest who had been the last incumbent to live in the chapel house before he retired to Ireland. She had asked him if he and his colleagues had ever experienced anything unusual in the house. His reply was, "We were always seeing things there!"

Some years later Professor Roy and I went to visit Peter and Jenny in their new home, also a council house. By this time they had two small children. We asked the couple to narrate, for my benefit, the account of events which took place in the chapel house those years before – which they did. When the man spoke again about the monk who threw him up in the air towards the ceiling, I realised that the fellow probably had an out-of-body experience caused by fright. The reason that I say this is that I asked him if he could see anything when he was on the "ceiling" to which he replied that he could see himself down below and the figure of the monk passing through him. It is very common for people to wish to make some kind of sense out of any occurrences such as these. After a review of past events we were told that all was peace and quiet in this new home and no such happenings had occurred again.

It was then I began to realise that this young mother looked awfully sad, pale and "out" of the conversation in some way. I was prompted intuitively to ask her if she was all right or if anything was on her mind that she wished to discuss.

She then told us that her 17 year old brother had committed suicide a few weeks previously, as he could not find work and things were looking bleak for him - at least in his eyes. He had hanged himself in the bathroom of his parents' house. It then transpired, through questioning, that *they* were hearing inexplicable raps and tapping noises coming from the shower rail in the bathroom of this new house. Once this statement was out in the open, the couple opened up and took on a different posture. Although the husband was a very tall man, certainly over 6 feet and physically well made, it became obvious that he was terrified to go into the bathroom on his own, even to use the toilet, and if he did so his wife had to stand outside the door until he came out again. When his wife pointed this out to us, he looked very embarrassed and nodded his head like a little boy to indicate that this was indeed true. I asked him why he was so afraid. He replied that he was scared that his wife's brother would build up and perhaps "appear" to him in the bathroom. This fear that someone you once knew and loved may appear in front of you is quite common in cases; personally I find that hard to understand, but then it hasn't happened to me. We all discussed the implications of the raps and taps and the possibility that perhaps the boy was only trying to let them know that he still maintained his intelligence, still existed in some way and that he had not totally left them behind. There was then a distinct difference in the appearance of the woman, the sister of the deceased boy; it was amazing; she brightened up, the colour came back into her face and in general she became more animated, joining in and now carrying the conversation.

I cannot honestly say that the husband was any more placated, but he could see the positive effect that this possibility was having on his wife and he was obviously pleased about that. We informed them that if they wanted us to come back with a sensitive we could do so, but quite often if it has been recognised by a household that someone is trying to communicate with them, that seems to be enough for the departed person. I always encourage people to wish that deceased person well and very often the phenomena will cease.

That is the way the situation was left, and we have heard no more about it. As with most things in life, no news is good news.

Old People's Homes

Residential homes for the elderly tend to throw up more than average numbers of reports of a paranormal nature. Perhaps in this type of situation we have ideal conditions for such phenomena to show themselves.

Possibly because:-

(a) The number of deaths over a period of time is much higher than that of an average house or building.

(b) It is more likely that those who have passed over are in a fairly confused and/or fragile condition, mentally and physically, and therefore could possibly find the "reality" (whatever that may mean) of their post mortem condition a problem.

Commonly reported phenomena in these types of homes include: people hearing footsteps when no one is there; the feeling of presence or that the shadow of a person has just passed by, but there is no one there when a person looks around; water in some form being turned on and off; electrical equipment operating of its own accord. Quite often the lifts in such buildings are favourites for self-operating. I should just stress here that these reports come from the staff and not usually the patients, although patients do appear to speak to invisible people from time to time, but this cannot always be treated as a psychical research matter.

In one residential home that I was asked to attend, as 'strange events' were reported, a new housekeeper was going about her business when she noticed a lady, in older style clothing, walking across the lounge, but she did not think anything of this until the lady "walked" through the wall at the other end of the lounge and disappeared. The lounge had other residents sitting around at the time but no one else, as far as we know, reacted to this event. This witness was totally shattered by the experience and became a gibbering wreck for some time after this. Even days later when a colleague and myself interviewed the woman, she did not appear too keen to speak with us at all at first as she was still so nervous and upset about the whole sequence of events. However as we spoke with her she settled down a bit when she realised that we were taking her seriously and really listening to her account. She had never seen, or believed in, anything like this before and yet again, as with many other people; she was struggling to come to terms with her experience.

In this same home, staff often saw a man standing in the garden, looking up at the building. He was dressed in an older fashioned style of clothing. This was actually the trigger that prompted the owner to call us in. After digging through the history of the building and its previous residents we felt that it was reasonable to conclude that the identity of this person was of a former butler from when it was a household residence.

Fortunately, after a time, most of the staff working in residential homes with regular "extras" just take it as a matter of course and know that there is nothing to fear or to worry about.

There can also be a humorous side to case investigations in old peoples' homes, although the participants might not think so at the time.

In the same home, already mentioned, the owner had a great understanding of the needs of people when they were about to pass and always tried to have someone with them at the point of death. A very elderly lady, we will call her Mary, who had no family or friends coming to visit, was very poorly; the doctor was sent for and he reinforced the thoughts of the nursing staff that she did not have long to live. This being the case, the owner sent a nurse to be with Mary in her private room and told her to take a new girl along with her. The new girl said, 'What will we do?' The owner replied, 'Keep it as natural as possible and just have an ordinary conversation.' The girls sat at each side of the bed and chatted to each other while Mary lay there, apparently in a coma-like state.

The doctor had said that it should not be too long until Mary passed. Meantime the owner phoned Mary's lawyer so that he could contact the graveyard people to have the ground softened in the family layer, as these events occurred during a spell of crisp winter weather.

After a while the nurse came back to the office and announced that Mary was now sitting up in bed. The owner thought that she was crazy and went along to the room to see for herself, where, much to her surprise, Mary was indeed sitting up in bed looking at her with a strange expression on her face. The owner smiled and said, 'Mary, where have you been?' The reply was, 'Well I don't know where I was, I seemed to be up a tunnel of some sort and I passed people that I didn't know and no one would speak to me. Then I heard these girls here talking about what they were going to have for lunch and one of them mentioned soup. I thought that sounded like a good idea and I just came back down the tunnel to join them.'

Mary lived another two years.

The following is another somewhat humorous account.

Two ladies had been companions in a residential home for several years and like all such companions there was a certain amount of envy between them over trivial matters. Soon after the passing of one of these ladies the other kept complaining to the staff that each morning her walking stick was missing and that "she" was taking it. This was, of course, referring to the recently deceased friend. The resident maintained that each night she would put her walking stick at the foot of her bed and each morning it would not be there, but subsequently it would be found in some other part of the building. She told the staff that one night she had awakened to actually see the deceased lady going off with her stick and she shouted at her to leave it alone. I have this lovely picture of the two of them fighting it out and wrestling over this peripatetic stick, but that's just my warped sense of humour.

In one particular room in the same home, there was a fairly new resident who, for weeks, appeared very surly and sour faced and who rarely smiled or showed much animation. However one morning she arrived at breakfast with her cheeks shining and wore a broad smile on her face. Every member of staff commented upon it. One person asked her how she was and how she was feeling, to which she replied that it was so nice that the lady in the tartan shawl had sat up with her all night and chatted about the old days and also gave her all the news about the residents in the home. Now this could have been dismissed as fantasy were it not for the fact that the previous resident of that particular room always wore a tartan shawl and she fitted the description given by the lady concerned. This lady would have no way of knowing that. No matter what conclusion you may come to, there is no doubt that this lady was greatly helped by her 'visits' from the lady with the tartan shawl. I have no doubt whatsoever that residential homes for the elderly will continue to provide investigators with material to examine for a long time to come.

Black

From experience, it would appear that poltergeist activity can be produced by a human being with latent negative emotional issues or from a discarnate source with various motives. As already indicated, when the activity is instigated by a discarnate source, it is normally a cry for attention and/or to let someone know that they are indeed 'there' in some way and that their essence still exists with the same personality, skills and memories still intact.

The next case is one in which I believe that the phenomenon produced was the product of stress and the power of the human mind. This relates to a lovely Roman Catholic lady who reported to me that she was seeing black furry animals scurrying around in her hallway, near the telephone table. No, it was not a case for rent-o-kill. The husband did not see these animals. A colleague and I made arrangements to meet with this lady and her husband in the College Club of Glasgow University and the following transpired.

The lady was obviously a very respectable and good living person who had a wonderful faith in her God. A slight problem arose here in our investigation as it transpired that there were two sets of strange events running side by side, which the family had lumped together in describing two types of phenomena as one. This turned out to innocently cloud their report, which resulted in the issues being inadvertently fudged somewhat in the beginning.

For some time, both she and her husband had often seen a figure of a "man" standing on the first floor landing on the bend of the internal stairs in their home. This man was usually smoking a pipe and smiling gently as he looked down at them as they stood in the lower hallway. He had a slightly transparent appearance.

After they had researched the recent history of the property it seemed sensible to conclude that he fitted the description of a previous owner of the house, although strangely enough not the last owner but the one before that. An interesting point to note is that this man's family and the present occupiers' family had quite a lot in common regarding family background and composition. Both were Roman Catholic families with two daughters, one of whom became a nun. I only give you this information as there may have been a point of affinity that in some way enabled the new residents to "observe" the previous owner, by some method unknown to us at this time.

When the black furry animals manifested themselves to the woman, the couple assumed that they were connected to the appearance of the gentleman, and they could not understand this as he appeared to be a fine old-fashioned gent with no sinister appearance whatsoever. After listening to their accounts of the events for over two hours, I was beginning to feel that we were not getting anywhere at all towards an understanding of them, or of finding a possible cause of this particular alleged phenomenon. There were no obvious signs of stress within this family. We searched, by questioning, into every avenue we could think of which may have been the cause, or a source of stress; no one had died recently, there were no financial problems, the relationship of the couple to each other seemed to be fine. We could not find any possible clue to give us direction.

Eventually I asked the lady, as she seemed to be the focus of the activity, if anything had caused her upset or resentment in the recent past. At first she said no, there was nothing – but I persisted with the question and then she hesitated, and indicated that there was an event a few months earlier that had upset her. The time factor fitted in with the appearance of the black furry animals, which, as I said, only she could see; but not her husband. Without revealing the lady's personal details, I can tell you that it transpired that the lady's father had abandoned her mother and herself when she was a baby and had taken himself off to Canada. A few months before our meeting she had received a phone call, out of the blue, from a Canadian female who said, "Your father is dead, he died a millionaire and you are not going to receive a penny."

We asked her how she felt about that, after the obvious shock of such a telephone call, if for example, did she then feel any strong negative emotions; at first she denied this but on reflection she realised that she was resentful and was holding this resentment to herself. At this point tears began to well up in her eyes and eventually rolled down her cheeks, actually – cascaded. The bubble had burst, and she cried and cried because she felt that she had "Let her God down" – her words. We talked her through the situation of her childhood and enabled her to feel sympathy for her father, who could not cope with the thought of the responsibility of a family at his very young age, and who ran away.

I pointed out that she had not let her God down, as she did not realise that she was doing this, but she might be thought to do so if she continued to hold the resentment towards her father. She entirely agreed.

After our meeting, the episodes with the black animals immediately ceased. One week later the lady telephoned to thank us for helping her to resolve her problem.

I deliberately wrote, *helping her to resolve her problem* as, without her recognition of the resentment built up within herself, I firmly believe that the activities would have continued, at least for some time. As it was, from that evening on, no further sightings of black furry animals took place.

The old gentleman still appeared from time to time, but this was not a problem.

It seems as though the product of the stress/resentment manifested itself in this peculiar way, by means unknown to us. To a person who has not examined paranormal phenomena this may sound absolutely crazy, but is it?

Let us consider the talent of Ted Serios who could project "pictures" onto photographic material, by staring into a camera lens. These were not airy-fairy shapes but distinct and easily recognised images, with some even produced in colour. After various forms of experimental methodologies, the investigative researchers of the time established that he could also produce a picture on the photographic material whether or not the camera had a lens in it.[3]

I mention this hopefully to make you think again about the immense power of the human mind and directed human thoughts. Certainly Serios must have projected his thoughts at a conscious level, whereas the lady who was seeing the black furry animals was operating at an unconscious or subconscious level.

And we don't even know how the mind does this.
If only we knew the dynamics of the operation!

---

[3] *The World of Ted Serios* by Jules Eisenbud

Bruises and scratches

In Glasgow, about ten years ago, Archie Roy and I attended a house which was quite near Barlinnie prison. I drove Archie out to a very nice semi-detached house where we met a very pleasant lady. She told us of some recent experiences that were causing her distress. She explained that she was not sleeping well because she felt as if she was being sexually interfered with in bed at night and, when she awakened in the morning, there would be bruises and scratches on her body, especially above her breasts. This had been going on for some time.

In these types of cases an investigator has to try to find out what has changed in a person's surroundings. This could be in any avenue of the person's life. The most common answer is that someone has died, but by no means is that the only trigger for the production of phenomena. Through questioning we established that the woman, who was in her early fifties, had lost her husband fairly recently and, since that time, had not really gone out of her house for anything. She had lost all of her confidence in leaving the house and had given up knitting, sewing and, to a great extent, cooking. Also present at the initial interview were two of her grown up children. During the interview other people came in and out of the lounge at various intervals to such an extent that they were interrupting the proceedings. During questioning the woman, let's call her Margaret, volunteered that one of her daughters had taken over the organisation of her weekly finances so much so that she, Margaret, was only left holding a purse with pocket money in it. It also became clear that she had never really had a chance to grieve properly for her husband as the family were always there – in her face, in her space – so to speak.

Due to all the interruptions I suggested that she and I would go upstairs to her bedroom and have a one to one chat. She readily agreed.

Even while we were upstairs her bedroom door kept opening and several individuals were coming in and out! I made sure that no one else would come in and I sat Margaret in a chair and just spoke quietly to her. I noticed that a photo of her husband was on her bedside table. I said to her, 'Do you say goodnight to him every night?' She did. I then said to her, 'I think that you just need a wee cuddle' and I put my arms around her neck from the back. That was it, the flood gates opened and she had a good cry. After that some colour returned to her face. I then talked her through a short colour meditation and gave her a structured routine to follow every night before she went to bed. One important point that I stressed was that no one else should ever come into her bedroom. In fact, I was actually providing her with some sort of control over her life.

Meantime Archie was downstairs talking to some other members of the family. He later said to me that he was somewhat concerned as the people would say things to each other such as, 'Is that the year that *** was up in the high court for murder?'

When I was upstairs with Margaret I found out that another possible factor in this case, in fact maybe the final trigger, was when two of her sons attacked each other with bats and knives right in front of her in the lounge. She ended up screaming at them and telling them forcefully to 'go away' – but not quite in those words.

All in all she was under a lot of stress.

As I said, we advised her to let no one else into her bedroom in the future as that was her space and she was in charge. She promised that she would do the colour meditation every night before she went to bed. I also suggested that she follow each meditation with a drink of water and a verbal 'goodnight' to her husband's picture.

We also strongly advised her to take control of her own money and left it at that.

As usual we happily gave permission for her to call us at any time subsequent to the visit. Two weeks passed and I had heard nothing from this woman. Curiosity got the better of me and I telephoned her. This is not something that I usually do. The conversation went something like this.

Me. Hi Margaret, Tricia here, how are you?

M. After a pause, 'Well I have a bit of a cold.'

Me . Thinking Eh? 'How are things in the house?'

M.'Fine. I'm going on holiday in a couple of months to see my sister in Canada.

(This is a woman who had not left the house for six months)

Me. 'Oh that's great, enjoy yourself.'

M. 'Thank you.'

There was no mention of any further phenomena. I was somewhat taken aback by her lack of reference to our previous meeting, but on reflection it is quite common after people have a resolution to an ostensible paranormal experience, for them not to want to talk about it once it has been resolved. I think that they are afraid that talking about it may bring it back. My conclusion is that subconsciously this woman was being mentally restricted by her family to such an extent that it was akin to rape. (Mental rape)

Once she took back control of certain situations in her life the stress appeared to be relieved.

Whatever the answer, the phenomena stopped and I have heard no more about this.

I am still holding to the idea that no news is good news.

Chapter 6

INSPIRATION

It interests me greatly that not only do we seem to be able to make ourselves known to the living after we die but we also appear to have a number of other seeming paranormal abilities while we are still alive. I would include in this number, topics such as telepathy, astral projection, remote viewing, dowsing, automatic writing, the gift of healing, knowing when people are staring at us, precognition, retrocognition – even just knowing when things are not quite right and receiving inspiration. Genius, it is said, is ten per cent inspiration and ninety per cent perspiration. To some, geniuses are eccentric, abnormal, nudging neighbours to madness.

The true story of genius is far removed from such ideas yet in itself is as strange and mysterious as any of these thoughts. Throughout the history of mankind geniuses have lived, creating their masterpieces in art, poetry, music, science and technology, philosophy, indeed in any of those creative spheres that have brought man up from the brute beast to some semblance of civilisation. While these inspired men and women have laboured, others have studied them and listened to these brilliant peoples' accounts of how they received their inspiration. Through such accounts runs a strange thread, leading to the extraordinary conclusion that it is common for men of genius to ascribe their inspirations for the most part to sources other than themselves. In case after case they claim that they are *given* their discoveries, their poems, their music, and their novels. One gets the decided impression that, far from being the creator or the managing director in their personality, they are no more than the public relations officer struggling to put across, after polishing and making ready for presentation, the material they have had thrust upon them.

This strange idea is best looked at by way of examples.

Goethe claimed that the songs he wrote made him, not he the songs.

As Frederic Myers put it: 'The influence rises from no discoverable source; for a moment it may startle or bewilder the conscious mind; then it is recognised as a source of knowledge, arriving through inner vision, while the action of the senses is suspended in a kind of momentary trance.'

George Sand, who also believed this with respect to her own work, also had the opportunity of seeing the composer Chopin struggling to get down on paper the wonderful theme that had come to him. She wrote: '(Afterwards) began the most heart-rending labour I ever saw. It was a series of efforts, of irresolutions, and of frettings to seize again certain details of the theme he had heard. He would shut himself up in his room for whole days, weeping, walking, breaking his pens, repeating and altering a bar a hundred times.'

George Frederich Handel was another composer who exemplified not only the power of inspiration but also the seeming remorseless drudgery it entailed to record perfectly the glorious music he received from the source. When given the libretto for "The Messiah" he retreated into his workroom and, hardly leaving it for any time, emerged after 24 days, shaken, on the verge of a nervous breakdown, but with the entire sublime music for "The Messiah" in his hand. He had, throughout this intense period of creation, largely sustained himself with cups of coffee.

Several men of genius have even talked about daemons, or brownies doing the original work and presenting it to them for final polishing. Kipling said that he had learned to trust his personal 'Daemon' for advice while Thackeray wrote: 'I have been surprised at the observations made by some of my characters. It seems as if an occult power was moving the pen.'

Robert Louis Stevenson obtained much of his most brilliant material from dreams. He also realised, as evidenced by his famous story of Dr Jekyll and Mr Hyde, that beyond the pool of light of a man's conscious personality lurked dark and sinister forces as well as the benevolent and clever entities he facetiously called his 'Brownies'.

Possibly the greatest thinker of all time, Socrates, was guided and advised in all his affairs by a voice, the so-called Daemon of Socrates. On many occasions he claimed that it warned him regarding certain courses of action he proposed to take and it was always right. The great philosopher acknowledged that whatever was the source of this intervention in his life, it was wiser than he and more knowledgeable. Socrates learned that all was well when the voice was silent and during the last days of his life, when his accusers sought his death, he drew strength and comfort from the fact that the voice intervened once only, to advise him against preparing any speech in his own defence.

Great scientists have also acknowledged the help they seemingly have been given in sleep or even in a waking state.

Friederich Kekule, the father of structural organic chemistry, after fruitless struggles concerning the nature of molecules, and in particular that of the benzene molecule, told how, on a London omnibus, he had a waking dream in which he had seen the atoms grouping themselves in patterns, snake-like, in space.

Lord Kelvin had a marked intuitive gift. Solutions came to him in a flash of inspiration and afterwards he had to labour consciously and exhaustively for proofs. Einstein, too, faced with a problem, seems to have had a definite vision of its solution. He remarked on this with $E = mc^2$. He said that one day he awoke – and it was there!

There are in fact too many cases – of geniuses claiming that their creative works are in some way given to them to polish and prepare for their fellow men – for us to doubt that they, in some strange way, are speaking the truth. However they put it, whether by using the terms Brownies or Daemons or 'subconscious mechanisms' or archetypes as in Jungian psychology, there seems to be a person or persons on the other side of the boundary to consciousness inspiring, teaching, guiding, desirous of helping them in their creative struggles. The term 'genius' is most aptly applied to those human beings, who have conscious abilities, that can mould and fashion what they have been given through inspiration into various forms.

Fairly recently I heard Paul McCartney, from the Beatles, say that one morning he awoke and one of his songs was just there – ready to write down. That song was 'Yesterday' and the title given to him was Scrambled Eggs. Thank goodness he changed it!

Professor William A. Lamberton, of the University of Pennsylvania, was studying a problem in descriptive geometry. After battling with the problem for almost two weeks he deliberately put it aside, knowing that in devoting more time to it he would merely bog himself still deeper in vain attempts.

He almost gave up his attempts at solving this problem – whose solution he had been seeking through the mathematical equations describing it. The solution, when it came, was along totally different lines. He woke one morning to see a geometrical figure apparently drawn on the north wall of his room, which had once been a classroom. The hallucination not only took the form of a geometrical statement of the problem but also had 'drawn' on it the auxiliary lines which demonstrated the solution. Professor Lamberton sprang from bed and drew the figure on paper. 'Needless to say,' he wrote afterwards, 'the geometrical solution being thus given, only a few minutes were needed to get the analytical one.'

It is also clear from the examples given that in most cases the man of genius has to do the spade-work himself, that is, his conscious personality has to sweat over the problem or work both before and after the 'person' on the other side intervenes. To that extent there is truth in the saying that genius is ten per cent inspiration and ninety per cent perspiration.

But 'where', if that is the correct word, does the source of inspiration of Rosemary Brown lie? She was only an elementary musician and yet claimed to have been receiving music by dictation since 1964, and would continue to receive until the mid-nineties. These were compositions from numerous composers, including Liszt, Beethoven, Bach, Schumann, Schubert, Brahms, Debussy and Rachmaninoff. She had had only a relatively elementary training in music and piano lessons. As time passed and the compositions continued to arrive, she wondered if she should try to improve her musical training in the hope of making it easier for the new compositions to come through and be recorded by her. The group of composers on the other side, claiming to be responsible for giving her the work, were strongly against this idea. "No," they said, "we are engaged in an enterprise to show humanity that death is a transition from one state to another wherein one retains one's individuality. If you take music lessons, it will make it easier for the sceptic to say that you yourself are composing these pieces."

There is no doubt that many distinguished musicians were impressed by what came through. Guy Lyon Playfair writes: '

> The general consensus was that while the music was not up to the standard of that written by the composers when alive, it was of a far

higher quality than could be expected even with somebody with considerably more musical training than she had ever had, and some of the music gave pause for thought.'

'Pianist Cristina Ortiz found one Chopin piece "absolutely incredible". Composer Richard Rodney Bennett admitted that, "I couldn't fake music like this Beethoven myself." Another composer, Liszt specialist Humphrey Searle, reckoned that an intricate piece called Grubelei, in which left and right hands must play five and three beats to the bar respectively (and in six sharps), "could well have been written by Liszt". It was in fact written, supposedly at Liszt's dictation, during a live BBC radio broadcast.'

Leading on from inspiration itself we have the phenomenon of automatic writing. In the previous examples most of the writers, musicians etc., had some desire or expertise within their areas but there are stranger events to come. There is, in my mind, a fine line between inspiration and other forms of information transfer and automatic writing. As usual in psychical research, nothing is ever simple and clear cut; definitions are at best difficult if not impossible and one phenomenon can blur into another. In the case of automatic writing many people have claimed that their hand, or a part of their consciousness, has been taken over and operated by 'someone else.' This may at first seem a little fanciful, until we look at some examples.

Chico Xavier.

This gentleman first came to my attention from the book *Chico Xavier, Medium of the Century,* by Guy Lyon Playfair, first published in 2010.

Chico was born in Brazil on the 2nd April 1910. He was educated only up to the sixth grade. In the year 2000, a Brazilian newspaper asked the general populous to vote for the Brazilian 'person' of the century, as they wished to commemorate that person by putting his face on a stamp.

Among those others nominated were a Brazilian known as 'the father of aviation', a former popular president and the very popular, if not iconic, football player Pelé. But who did the populous vote for? Chico Xavier, a shop assistant whose father was illiterate!

Why?

This man had the gift of automatic writing. Even as a child he could hold a pencil over a blank sheet of paper and produce words and sentences which could not have been written by him from the reserves of his own vocabulary. By the year 2002 he had written by automatic writing 458 books, sales of which had passed the 50 million mark. The content of these works was staggeringly *vastly* beyond his educational level and understanding.

Since 1927 he had spent 5 hours a day contacting his spirit guides.

In a book of poems, penned by Xavier, called *Parnassus*, there are 259 poems signed by 56 different poets. This included almost every leading figure from Brazilian and Portuguese poetry. These poems were given the stamp of authenticity by those in the know.

Throughout his life he donated all of the money earned from the books to charity – he never took a penny. Being interested in the possible workings of the phenomenon himself he took part, incognito, in an electro-encephalograph test, both in and out of trance, with fascinating results.

In simple terms it showed that a different part of his brain was in use when he was writing automatically. In actual fact, because the session was a 'blind' test to the operators of the equipment, they stated that the two results were obviously not from the same person.

Just after one of Chico's books was published, an admirer brought along to him a copy of a book written by an eminent scientist, Hermani Andrade, who was also interested in spiritual matters. Andrade approached these things from a more scientific standpoint. The person asked Chico's opinion of Andrade's book. His reply was, 'How would I know – I couldn't even understand my own!'

Chico did so much for the people in his area that he was respected and loved. He was modest and never sought fame, and remember – he never took a penny for himself but used the money for the good of the community.

Whatever else Chico was he was one hundred percent genuine. As for the modus operandi of automatic writing, who really knows?

Patience Worth

Most of you will never have heard of the name Patience Worth, why should you?

Only people who have a reasonable background in psychical research would know of her and yet...to this day...'her' identity still remains a mystery.

You have heard the saying that fact is stranger than fiction and this is certainly true in this example.

In Missouri around the beginning of 1913, a Mrs Pearl Curran and some other ladies met regularly to operate a Ouija board. My warning; do not try this yourself. The sessions produced the usual bland so-called communications from deceased friends and relatives, most probably from the unconscious minds of the sitters. But in July of that year something completely different occurred. The board spelt out; *Many moons ago I lived. Again I come —Patience Worth my name. Wait I would speak with thee. If thou shalt live, then so shall I. I make my bread at thy hearth.* From then until December 1937 this communicator 'used', if that is the correct word, Mrs Curran to produce amazing poems, prayers, prose and plays.

Mrs Curran had an elementary education and left school at 14. She was a bright woman of higher than average intelligence but was not at all well educated in poetry, prose, plays or even history.

Patience Worth had a completely different personality from Mrs Curran, being humorous and very quick-witted, we might even say cheeky. She said that she was born in Dorset in 1649 or 1694. I am not sure why there is this discrepancy on the dates.

During the time of this alliance there was quite an outpouring of original literature. This was achieved through the Ouija board and later supplemented by Mrs Curran's spoken word and I do believe later by a form of automatic writing.

There were four novels produced: *The Sorry Tale, Telka, Hope Trueblood* and *The Pot upon the Wheel.* All in all Mrs Curran's total output over the years was in the region of three million words. This did not include the conversations that she had with people such as journalists, academics, medical men, etc., who came to meet and question her. In these situations her quick-witted retorts really came into play.

Dr Walter Franklin Prince was one such visitor to her *hearth.* After questioning Patience for a time, via Mrs Curran, Prince said, 'You are a continuing subconscious dream of Mrs Curran.'

> **Patience:** *And what be thee, Sirrah? Nay, egad – thee art a sorry dream – over too much curd.*

This quick-witted discourse continued for some time and often the replies were a millisecond after Prince's question or observation.

Sometime later into the 'interrogation' the following occurred.

Prince to Patience: *Part of the odd words you use, she (Mrs Curran) unconsciously remembers, others she has invented.*

Patience: *Well, it be a trick – can thee do it?*

The Sorry Tale, although a novel, displayed a great detailed knowledge of Roman and Jewish customs and incorporated characters like Jesus, Augustus Caesar and Herod. The second novel, Telka, showed a wide knowledge of medieval England. Remember that Mrs Curran was American.

In February 1926, Prince, with no warning, asked Patience to write lines beginning with all the letters of the alphabet, except x, in the correct order. The reply came, fully in alphabetical order, minus x, at a speed which was difficult to take down even in shorthand. Prince himself later remarked dryly that her opinion of the task to which she was set is evident from the last two lines.

Yea, this thy servant upon the path of folly
Zealously endeavouring that she follow a fool.

Mrs Curran died on the 3rd December 1927 and at her funeral a friend quoted something that Patience had said: *What a paltry pence is death to buy eternity; what a light price to pay for an everlasting abiding place.*

The sceptical Dr Prince argued for and against every theory presented for the Patience phenomenon and found none really acceptable.

His last words in his case study of Patience were:

'Either our concept of what we call the subconscious must be radically altered, so as to include potencies of which we hitherto have had no knowledge, or else some cause operating through but not originating in the subconsciousness of Mrs Curran must be acknowledged.'

But when does inspiration become automatic writing or genius and when do these extra talents prompt the thought: 'Could this be a talent from potential reincarnation?' Where can we draw lines? Where, for example, does the inspiration or talent come from that influences a young child who can barely speak; if indeed inspiration is the correct word on this occasion. Let us look at the strange case of Jay Greenberg,

Jay Greenberg

Jay Greenberg is a young man, born in 1991 in New Haven, Connecticut, who studied at New York City's Julliard School of music. Neither parent was or is a professional musician; his father is a linguist and his mother a painter. When he was around two years of age he voluntarily drew a cello and wrote the word cello. His mother was more than surprised as no one in the family had anything to do with string instruments and she wouldn't have expected him to know what a cello was. He later asked her for a cello as he "knew" that he wanted one. His mother then took him to a music shop where he was shown a miniature cello, which he immediately held and started to play. She was astounded. By the age of three he was still drawing cellos, but had turned them into notes on a scale and was beginning to compose original music.

As time passed his compositions became faster and faster until he was composing anywhere and at any time. His father said that Jay hears music in his head all of the time and the boy actually became a problem at elementary school as teachers did not know how to deal with the situation.

Jay[4] has exceptionally keen hearing – many times more sensitive than an average person. He can block out the sounds of the physical world around him, but he cannot switch off the music in his head. He explained that he often hears more than one new composition at a time and that his brain is able to control two or three new pieces of music at the same time. He describes them as channels of music. (I imagine like tuning into various radio stations.) This is, of course, along with the channel of everyday life.

By the age of ten, Jay was at Julliard, among the world's top conservatories of music.

By eleven, he was studying music theory with third year college students.

One of his piano tutors noted that Jay wrote things that he couldn't even play and when asked to describe the process of his writing he said that he "hears" a tune, listens to it and then he starts humming

---

[4] http://www.jaygreenbergmusic.com

it and then, while walking, he walks to the beat and often starts conducting as well.

When he was around twelve years of age he took a Beethoven sonata and transposed it backwards and upside down. Even his teacher couldn't follow it. He actually took the clefts and inverted them, the treble became bass, bass became treble and, as I said, he did it backwards.

Talented composers might write five or six symphonies in a lifetime, but Jay had written five by the age of twelve. An outstanding feature of his work is the fact that he rarely, if ever, revises a composition. This is in complete contrast to many outstanding composers whose manuscripts are sometimes difficult to read due to all the changes that were made during the composing process.

By the age of 14 he had composed more than 100 musical works, including five symphonies, seventeen piano sonatas and five piano concertos. Jay's Fifth Symphony is highly acclaimed and was released on the Sony Classical label on August 15th 2006, with Jose Serebrier conducting the London Symphony Orchestra. The Orchestra of St Luke's commissioned Jay Greenberg to write a one movement violin concerto for Joshua Bell, which was premiered at Carnegie Hall on 28th October 2007.

Now what are we to make of this case and others in this chapter?

Inspiration?
Genius?
Possession?
Reincarnation?

Whatever the answer it is difficult to come to any conclusions. Regarding Jay, some people will trot out the word *savant*: a person with a particular island of intelligence or ability in one particular area.

To me this is not always a suitable explanation. Why was a three year old child able to pick up a cello and, without any training or exposure to that instrument, immediately be able to play it?

Yet again, the complexities and vagaries of psychical research and philosophical arguments make one comprehensive theory almost impossible.

Nevertheless, although no definite answer can be given, there are many clues leading to a tentative 'model' of genius, inspiration and automatic writing. It must be accepted that our conscious personality is little more than a fraction of the human psyche or personality and that most of that psyche is outside consciousness. Frederick Myers called those other reaches of personality the subliminal; that is to say, the parts below the threshold of consciousness. A limited definition of the subliminal or unconscious is that it contains everything – for example our memories – that is not held within consciousness. But, as Myers, William James, Jung and indeed all those who have truly appreciated the complexity of human personality have taught, the subliminal is much, much more than that. It merges with something that has been termed the collective unconscious which belongs to all men. The evidence that a person's personality both conscious and unconscious is not a closed system is provided by telepathy, clairvoyance, ostensible cases of possession such as those seen in the trance states of mediums. The inspiration of genius, then, is but another source of evidence of the existence of this great uncharted psychic/spiritual continent which, for its own purposes, interacts with mankind in many forms. These things happened and we have to provide some sort of ongoing theory, even if it turns out eventually to be wrong. As Augustus De Morgan wrote in 1863 in his preface to *From Matter to Spirit*, xxiv. London: Longman, Roberts and Green: 'Facts have sometimes started a theory, but until sagacity had conjectured, divined, guessed, surmised what they pointed to, the facts were a mob and not an army.'

Chapter 7

OBSESSION

Unless a person has researched topics such as this, there is no use in dismissing them as nonsense, without inquiry. The same may be said of course for any paranormal, or even 'normal', subject. Overshadowing, or inspiration, occurs when a person feels that their actions are being affected by an outside influence. As we have seen, it is very common for poets, artists, musicians and others to say that their work has actually been given to them or influenced by other sources, but obsession is slightly different.

Obsession occurs when a person is obsessed in one particular avenue of their life, carrying out tasks that they would not normally attempt. The person often displays skills, sometimes acquired overnight, that they did not have before. One of the best examples of obsession is the Thompson–Gifford case, where the goldsmith Frederick Thompson was suddenly obsessed with painting landscapes, to the detriment of his own business, when in fact he had no training whatsoever in painting. The paintings were quite magnificent and after a time were recognised as being in the style of Robert Swain Gifford who had died six months before the onset of Thompson's obsession. For the rest of his life Thompson continued to paint.[5]

---

[5] The full account of this may be found in the proceedings of the American S.P.R by Professor Hyslop 1909 or in *The Archives of the Mind* SNU Publications, by Professor Archie Roy 1996.

So, what were the circumstances that brought this about?

In the summer of 1905 a bizarre series of events began in the life of Frederic Lewis Thompson, a successful goldsmith working in New York City, married, thirty-six years of age and seemingly settled in his career. He was suddenly and inexplicably seized with an uncontrollable urge to sketch and paint pictures, not of scenes that he chose but of vivid hallucinations floating before him of trees and landscapes. His oil paintings showed a most unusual power of technique and composition, far beyond anything a beginner should have been able to produce. One painting, a stand of gnarled trees, surprised him by its quality; it was almost as if it painted itself. He lost total interest in his work as a goldsmith. Sometimes he would say to his bewildered and worried wife: *"Gifford wants to sketch"* for at those times he felt that he was the American landscape artist Robert Swain Gifford. His wife was very concerned and beginning to wonder if he had lost his rationale.

Thompson had a very slight acquaintance with this man, Gifford. He knew that the latter was much older than he was, having come across him once or twice in the marshes about New Bedford when Gifford had been sketching and Thompson had been out hunting. On another occasion he had called upon Gifford in New York to show him some jewellery but thereafter saw nothing more of him.

Some months later, in January 1906, he saw a notice stating that an exhibition of the late R. Swain Gifford's paintings would be held at the American Art Galleries. While there he suffered a new hallucination, an auditory one. A voice said: "You see what I have done. Can you not take up and finish my work?"

During 1906 Thompson painted even more assiduously than before, producing some works of such high quality that they sold on their artistic merit alone. But he and his wife Carrie were growing ever more worried, for both feared that he was losing his mind as his compulsion was now so overwhelming that he was painting in states of mind ranging from slight dissociation to almost complete automatism. No longer capable of working as a goldsmith, his financial situation was becoming precarious. In this new state he sought medical help. Not only did Gifford seem to be inspiring him but controlling and obsessing him to continue his work. The original personality of Thompson still existed but he, in some way, was impelled to carry out the work of a deceased personality, namely Gifford.

He was fortunate in that his medical man did not conclude that his strange story was due to insanity. He referred Thompson to Professor

James H. Hyslop (1854 - 1920),[6] professor of logic and ethics at Columbia University, secretary and executive head of the American Society for Psychical Research. Thompson visited Hyslop on January 16th, 1907. Hyslop noted that Thompson's story recalled cases investigated by the Society for Psychical Research where the percipients were not mentally disturbed but had suffered some form of paranormal intrusion. Thompson agreed to accompany Hyslop to a medium, Mrs Maggie Gaule, although Thompson himself thought the whole subject of spiritualism was utterly ridiculous. Mrs Gaule was told nothing and Thompson was merely introduced to her as a Mr Smith.

The statements that she made marked the beginning of an extraordinary series of visits to a number of mediums and an intensive investigation by Hyslop and Thompson to make sense of Thompson's obsession. This led Thompson to visit several islands including various members of the Elizabeth Islands, off Buzzard's Bay, Massachusetts and Naushon Island, where Gifford was born, in an attempt to identify the scenes in some of the paintings he was being obsessed to carry out. Sometimes Hyslop accompanied him. The mediums gave a large number of veridical statements, far too many to be attributed to chance and a scenario was composed by them of a painter, resembling Gifford, specialising in landscape and wooded works, who allegedly said, "I will help you, because I want someone who can catch the inspiration of these things as I did, to carry on my work." Various idiosyncrasies that Gifford had while working were given correctly. Descriptions of his two studios, one in the country and one in the city, were also accurate. Descriptions were given of the scenes he had painted, with detailed instructions on how to find the locations.

Two and a half years after Gifford's death, Thompson paid a visit to the artist's widow. Mrs Gifford kindly allowed him to see her late husband's studio, which had not been greatly altered since his death. Thompson's shock and emotional turmoil were intense as he saw on an easel an unfinished sketch identical to one of those he had left with Hyslop more than a month before. In addition, he saw on other easels two different pictures, identical to sketches he had previously made. They were no casual or rough resemblances as the scenes, even to the composition of small stands of trees and the contours of their branches, simply could not be attributed to coincidence.

Hyslop later obtained Mrs Gifford's testimony that the first picture

---

[6] Hyslop 1909 PASPR 3, 1-469, A Gauld, PSPR 55 273-340.

had been rolled and put away until after her husband's death, when it was taken out and put on the easel. Therefore Thompson would have had had no previous opportunity to see it.

Subsequently on his visit to Nashawana Island he found the exact scene of Gifford's picture that had haunted him. On another island he came across more scenes that he had already painted. While there he made some fresh paintings and sketches. As he was sketching a group of trees, he heard a voice in his head say, 'Go and look on the other side of the tree.' He did so and found Gifford's initials carved into the bark of a beech tree. Hyslop himself photographed them two months later. They were 'long grown up and could not have been cut by Mr Thompson.' Indeed Hyslop by this time felt that Thompson's veracity was no longer in question. Hyslop's list of people who vouched for many of Thompson's statements was now a long one; in addition he had also been impressed by the information given to Thompson and himself by the mediums that they had consulted.

As a result of all this information Hyslop arranged for new sittings with mediums to take place. They provided a great deal of additional strikingly relevant information, much of it could possibly have been gained by telepathy on the part of the mediums, but some of it was extremely difficult to attribute to extrasensory perception involving living people. Space forbids more detail: I can only urge interested readers to consult for example Hyslop's comprehensive paper in the Proc. ASPR (Hyslop, 1909), with the warning that it is 469 pages long.

Frederic Thompson continued to paint into his later years, never going back to his goldsmith's business. The psychical researcher D. Scott Rogo found that he followed a career as an artist, taking a studio in New York. In the summer of 1922 several of Thompson's paintings appeared in an exhibition of psychically inspired paintings and sketches.

By 1927, Thompson, still a painter, was living in Miami. He never denied the Robert Swain Gifford origin of his artistic beginnings and maintained throughout his life that he still received inspiration from him. Thompson probably died sometime between 1927 and 1935.

Although he called it inspiration, I would say that he was originally obsessed by Gifford to carry out the work. He had no conscious desire to do this and, you will remember, at one point both he and his wife were concerned for his sanity.

Hardly a benign act I feel.

Chapter 8

POSSESSION

In possession, unlike obsession, the normal personality – the host – appears to be completely displaced by an intruding personality. While the intruder is present, there is no trace of the host's personality. It is interesting to note that the host's normal skills, memories and other personal information also appear to be inaccessible to the incoming personality, the intruder therefore unable to use them. However, the incoming personality can appear to be accompanied by his/her own skills, memories and personal information. In cases of this kind, when the host returns to normal consciousness that person's normal skills, memories and information are once again accessible; we call this type of case one of intermittent, or temporary, possession. If the host does not return to normal consciousness during the lifetime of the person's body, that type of case would be classified as one of permanent possession: possibly akin to a computer being controlled by a completely different operating system and program.

The case of Jasbir Lal Jat

In Rasulpur in 1954 little Jasbir Lal Jat[7], who was three and a half years old, died of smallpox. His father, Sri Girdhari Lal Jat suggested

<hr />

[7] *20 Cases Suggestive of Reincarnation* (second edition 1974) Charlottesville, University press of Virginia. I Stevenson.

to the village elders that, as custom dictated, the body should immediately be buried, as smallpox was an infectious illness. The elders, however, said that as it was night and dark, the burial should be carried out in the morning. The grieving father returned to his house and sat down beside the body of his child. To his astonishment, after a time, he saw a tremor pass through the child's body. His son was not dead. An intensity of careful nursing gradually, after many days, brought the child out of his death coma and ultimately he made a full recovery; with an astonishing and perplexing unforeseen consequence.

Once the little boy was able to speak again he told his family that he was Sobha Ram, the son of Shankar, who lived in Vehedi village and he wanted to go home. He also stated that he was a Brahmin and insisted on the correct Brahmin food. He refused to eat any food that his family prepared and would only eat when the parents were able to prevail upon a Brahmin neighbour to bring food in for him. The troubled parents were unable to shake his claim. He told them that he had taken part in a wedding, that he had eaten some poisoned sweets, had fallen off a ceremonial chariot, hit his head on the ground and been fatally injured. He asked, 'What am I doing here?' Summing up this very carefully investigated case by Professor Ian Stevenson, it was found that the child's story about Sobha Ram and the circumstances of his death were true. Members of the Sobha Ram family, including Sobha Ram's father, travelled to Rasulpur about three years after the boy's recovery from smallpox. When the child first met this family he recognised them and gave their exact relationships to Sobha Ram.

He was then, with witnesses, allowed to travel to Vehedi. When they arrived there he was asked to lead the way to Sobha Ram's house and he did so without hesitation. He remained in Vehedi for some days and showed that he possessed a detailed knowledge of the family and its affairs, recognising a considerable number of people and showing that he knew their exact relationship to him. When a younger cousin of Sobha Ram entered a room where 'Jasbir' was, the little boy said 'Come in Gandhiji.' Someone present said, 'This is Birbal.' The boy replied, 'We call him Gandhiji.' a nickname Birbal had because he had large ears and bore a resemblance to Mahatma Gandhi. 'Jasbir' showed particular interest in a little boy named Baleshwar which was not surprising as the child was the son of Sobha Ram. While in Vehedi, he and Baleshwar slept together in the same cot, which was customary for father and son, but not strangers.

In 1961 Stevenson visited both Vehedi and Rasulpur and interviewed thirteen witnesses to the case. Both families stated that before the case arose they had never heard of each other. Stevenson returned in 1964 and reviewed the case, using new interpreters and interviewing additional witnesses. In 1971 he again visited India and re-examined the case, interviewing 'Jasbir' who was now a young man of about twenty-two who was still insistent by statement and actions that he was Sobha Ram.

Sobha Ram certainly died about the same time that Jasbir went into his 'death' coma in 1954. This cannot be a case of reincarnation as the boy was three and a half when Sobha Ram died. It is more consistent with a case of permanent possession where the normal personality is displaced entirely by an intruder. Jasbir's body was as near death as a body can be and still remain alive. Sobha Ram's body was dead. Sobha Ram said (through Jasbir) that immediately after he died he was sort of floating about, who knows where, when he met a man of some kind who said to him, 'That child down there is dying, if you are quick you can take his body.' It would be interesting to know exactly when the transformation took place but it is impossible to say with certainty as Jasbir was barely alive for many weeks after he began to recover and before he could speak again.

What we can say is that at the age of 22, the boy Sobha Ram, who appears to have 'filled' the body of Jasbir Lal Jat and who had passed through a strange and terrible experience had grown into a mature self-confident young man on affectionate terms with both of his families, accepting his lot and prepared to make the most of his second time around.

We can only observe, document and assess wherever we can.

I reiterate: possession cases can be divided into two categories-permanent and temporary/intermittent.

Permanent
Example 1: The case of Jasbir Lal Jat, as above.

The original personality of Jasbir never returned.

There are other cases of possession where the intruder has been present for over twenty years, the host absent throughout this period of time, and yet the original personality may make a fleeting return.

Example 2: Outline of the Sumitra - Shiva Tripathi case.[8]

After a series of deep fits of unconsciousness that seemingly brought her close to death, the poorly educated Sumitra's personality disappeared. It was replaced on return to consciousness by the Shiva Tripathi personality, that of a well-educated woman, who died six months before the personality transfer. This 'intruder', the Shiva personality, was then in possession of Sumitra's body for many years except, bizarrely, for a short episode of a few hours when the host personality of Sumitra once briefly 'surfaced.'

Intermittent

Example 1: Outline of the Uttara Huddar - Sharada case.

A Bengali speaking woman, Sharada, from the 1800's has been appearing through Uttara Huddar, a university lecturer, at intervals for almost thirty years, staying for periods of a few days to a few weeks. Whatever she learns to do during a visit, when she is in control of the body, she retains that knowledge, or skill, and is able to use it during her subsequent appearances. She does not appear to have automatic access to any information known by Uttara or indeed any skills that Uttara has mastered. As far as I know this situation continues right up to the present day. The strange thing is that the University gives Uttara 'absence of leave' whenever Sharada takes over her body.

Example 2: Outline of the Watseka Wonder case.

In the Watseka Wonder case, Mary Roff, who died when Lurancy Vennum[9] was eighteen months old, took over Lurancy's body when Lurancy was in her early teens and stayed in control for three months. The Mary Roff personality recognised Mary's relatives, identified possessions belonging to Mary and recalled many incidents in Mary's past. There was then a return of Lurancy. Thereafter, throughout the rest of Lurancy's life, there was a number of occasions when Mary's personality returned for a very short time.

---

[8] Sumitra Singh – Stevenson et al 1989, *Journal of Scientific Exploration,* 3,81-101.

[9] R Hodgson, *Religio-Philosophical Journal,* Dec 20th 1890. JSPR 10, 1901.

An additional phenomenon was common to two of these four cases, Sumitra and Watseka, namely the intrusion of identifiable transient personalities before the main 'intruder' took hold. This should give us a lot of food for thought.

To understand more clearly why many psychical researchers attach such importance to cases such as these, I append more relevant details about them.

In the Sumitra-Shiva Tripathi case, it was early in 1985 that Sumitra began to suffer spells of unconsciousness or trance. In this condition her eyes would roll upwards and her teeth would be clenched, the episodes varying in duration from a few minutes to a day. In two of them she seemed to be taken over by different personalities. One said she was a woman from Sharifpura (the village where Sumitra lived with her husband) who had drowned herself in a well. Another claimed that he had been a man in a different Indian state. During one of these trance-like states in July, she predicted that she would die in three days. On the predicted day she did appear to die and her grieving relatives began to make preparations for her funeral. Nevertheless she was not dead and, after the passage of a period of time in this state of apparent death, she recovered. The word 'she' is perhaps inappropriate as on recovery the basically educated Sumitra was found to have disappeared. She was replaced on return to consciousness by the Shiva Tripathi personality, that of a well-educated woman whose life, as I said, was cut short six months before this event. This person had the ability to write fluent letters to Shiva's family relatives. She displayed a complete knowledge of Shiva's life in her husband's in-laws' house in the town of Dibiyapur. She also had a wide knowledge of the Tripathi's family, who lived in Etawah where she had received her excellent education.

If we turn now to the well documented Watseka Wonder case, we learn that Mary Roff, who lived in Watseka, died in 1865. Another girl, called Lurancy Vennum, was fifteen months old at this time. Lurancy was born in April 1864 in Milford Township, about seven miles from Watseka, Illinois. When Lurancy was about three months old the family moved to Iowa, returning to the vicinity of Watseka in October 1865. This was about three months after the death of the 19 year old Mary Roff, who had suffered severe fits from the age of six months. Some of these fits were extremely violent and during her short lifetime became increasingly worse. She also had episodes of despondency and in one of these, in July 1864, she cut her arm with a knife until she fainted. At the beginning of the last year of her life, one such fit caused her to suffer five days of raving mania, although she temporarily recovered. It was during another of these fits that she died in July 1865.

When, years later, the other girl, Lurancy, began to exhibit her own strange behaviour, her family was living at a considerable distance from the Roffs, their houses being on opposite sides of Watseka. The two families had previously only the slightest acquaintance with each other when, during the summer of 1871, the Vennum family lived about 200 yards from Mr Roff's house. One visit was made by Mrs Roff to Mrs Vennum and the two men had merely a formal speaking acquaintance. Up until July 1877, Lurancy had enjoyed good health. Some days before the major phenomena began she told her family, 'There were persons in my room last night: and they called "Rancy! Rancy!" and I felt their breath on my face.' The next night she left her bed, protesting that she could not sleep because every time she tried to sleep she heard voices calling "Rancy! Rancy!"

This episode was followed a few days later by Lurancy suffering some kind of fit after which she lay unconscious for five hours. The next day, July 12, she had another which led to her announcing that she could see heaven and angels and people whom she knew had died, including a little brother and sister. These incidents, in which she seemed almost entranced, continued until the end of January 1878. These fits, together with her wild statements, persuaded onlookers that she was insane, most saying that she should be committed to an asylum.

Early in 1878, Mr and Mrs Roff, who had heard about the case, suggested to the Vennums that they should call in Dr E.W. Stevens of Janesville, Wisconsin. They agreed and on January 31st, Dr Stevens and Mr Roff called upon the Vennums. Lurancy appeared to be possessed by a number of entities one after the other, including an old woman called Katrina Hogan and a man called Willie Canning. At first the girl looked like 'an old hag', sitting in a chair by the stove, elbows on her knees, hands under her chin, feet curled up on the chair. During this period she acted sullen and crabbed, called her father 'Old Black Dick' and her mother 'Old Granny'. She did however talk with Dr Stevens and stated that he would understand her. It was then that she claimed to be Katrina Hogan. The transition to Willie Canning then took place. A fit followed some irrational conversation and, with a great deal of effort, Dr Stevens managed to hypnotise her. The girl calmed down and claimed that she had been controlled by evil spirits. She also said that there was a spirit who wanted to control her and gave its name as Mary Roff. Mr Roff exclaimed, "That is my daughter: Mary Roff is my girl. Why, she has been in heaven twelve years. Yes, let her come, we'll be glad to have her come."

The consequence of this entreaty by Mr Roff was that within twenty-four hours, Mary Roff had ostensibly possessed Lurancy Vennum's body. She stayed for three months, most of that time living with the Roff family, behaving exactly as their daughter would have done, identifying relatives who visited the house, recognising possessions that had been Mary's and recalling many incidents in Mary's past. Thereafter, the Mary Roff personality left, allowing Lurancy to return and be restored to the Vennum family. Throughout the rest of Lurancy's life, which was for the most part a normal one, there were short returns of Mary's personality almost like a person visiting a friend.

In some possession cases we often find it difficult or indeed impossible to discover a convincing point of affinity between the host and an intruding personality. In the four well-authenticated cases of Sumitra, Lurancy Vennum, Jasbir Lal Jat and Uttara Huddar,[10] the Vennum case is the only one where a reasonable link is apparent; namely the fact that the Roff parents had previously met and spoken with the Vennum parents, they lived in the same town of Watseka, both Mary and Lurancy suffered from somewhat similar kinds of illness, and Dr Stevens treated both girls.[11]

The other three cases reveal no obvious signs of points of affinity linking possessor to the possessed. Sobha Ram, the possessor, died after the fall from the ceremonial chariot about the time when Jasbir Lal Jat, the 'host', went into his apparent death coma. Shiva Tripathi, the possessor, died about six months before Sumitra, the 'host', appeared to die. Sharada, the possessor, died almost one and a half centuries before Uttara Huddar, the 'host', was born. A curious feature in those cases is that the three possessors did not seem to have any intention in taking over the respective possessed bodies. Both Shiva Tripathi and Sharada, finding themselves in other bodies, were bewildered and terrified at first and denied the reality of their new situation. In Sobha Ram's case, he maintained that when he found that he had died and was 'elsewhere', a sadhu (a holy man or saint) advised him to 'take cover' in the body of Jasbir, son of Girdhari Lal Jat. He was certainly not satisfied with his new existence, trapped in

[10] V. V. Akolkar 1992, JASPR, 86,209-247

[11] Stevens, E.W. (1887), Hodgson, R. (1890), Myers, F.W.H., (1903), Roy, A.E. (1996, 2005)

a small boy's body and he continually expressed a desire to be taken to Sobha Ram's family.

A further curious and significant feature in all four cases is that the possessed were 'out of it' for some time before the possession, in markedly abnormal states. Sumitra and Jasbir Lal Jat were judged to be dead by witnesses. Lurancy was suffering from increasingly severe fits, often accompanied afterwards by wild statements. Even Uttara Huddar had spent a considerable time in a severe psychologically troubled and unhappy state, employing deep meditation and breathing exercises and practising automatic writing before Sharada made her first bewildered appearance.

Again, when we look at the ages of the possessors when they died, we find that their lives were cut short. When they died, Mary Roff was almost nineteen, Shiva Tripathi was twenty-two, Sharada was twenty-four and Sobha Ram was twenty-six. In addition Shiva had two young children, Sharada was pregnant with her first child and Sobha Ram had a young son Baleshwar, therefore perhaps giving them the will to still be with their families.

If we again turn our attention to the possessed, we find that the age at which their personalities were 'ejected' was 14 for Lurancy; Sumitra was 17, Jasbir was three and a half while Uttara was 33 years of age.

But all this, while interesting and very possibly significant, does not help us to understand why, apart from the Vennum case, these particular incomers became possessors of the respective 'host' bodies. Was it just some bizarre chance?

Investigators and students of the Sharada case, such as professors Akolkar, Pal, Pasricha and Stevenson have examined not only the possession hypothesis but also assessed how well reincarnation, cryptomnesia, fraud, super-ESP and even multiple personality could fit the case. In their well-argued assessments they consider reincarnation and possession to be the only plausible hypotheses. The reader is urged to study their papers not only to realize how seriously they take this case but how carefully and minutely they have weighed up every detail in coming to their conclusions.

The universe is not only queerer than we imagine; it is queerer than we can imagine.

—J.B.S.HALDANE

Chapter 9

REINCARNATION

Reincarnation is different from possession in that, from the age when a child can speak, he/she speaks of memories of living in a different place and of having different parents and is adamant that this was his/her life. In other words there is no alteration to the original personality. Often the identity of the former life spoken about can be found if details are specific enough.

As previously stated The University of Virginia has over 3,000 such cases. To dismiss the idea that these things all happened in the dim and distant past, I will give you a modern example.

Sonam

Sonam was a little girl from the village of Broda. She was born on the 12th May 2007. As soon as she could speak, she spoke of a former life in which she lived in the village of Batta.

This case came to the attention of two investigators, Dr Madan Parmarand and Dr Kuldip Dhiman, who managed to get permission to call at the girl's family home in 2011.

They verified that from when she could string a sentence together, she maintained that she had been Mukesh Kumar from Batta and that he was a soldier. When asked what Mukesh did for a living she would use her hands to make the action of firing a gun and say, *di-shoom... dishoom!*

When asked how she (he) died she would say, *fauji dakus did dishoom.*

Being such a small child she could not provide any more information.

The adults in her life tried to find out more about these words and the best interpretation and explanation that they could come up with at the time was *terrorist.*

In fact it was subsequently found out that Mukesh had actually died after being allegedly hit by a train, but Sonam said that she (he) had been shot and later pushed under a train.

She said that five or six *fauji dakus* had shot her and there was speculation that it was people from her (his) own army who shot her (him).

In Hindi *fauji* means soldier and *daku* means bandit.

As a point of interest, Sonam said that Mukesh had been shot in the chest and indeed she had a small red birthmark in the centre of her chest. (This may or may not be relevant, of course, but worth noting.)

Dr Dhiman later checked with army friends and found out that the term *fauji daku* is also used to describe soldiers who kill their fellow soldiers.

This case came to light when a woman from Batta visited Broda and heard rumours about a girl who claimed to be a soldier from Batta. After some inverstigation, the identity of Mukesh was verified and people contacted Mukesh's family. This family then agreed to visit Sonam in her own village.

When she, now 4, met her 'previous' family, she rushed up to them and eagerly hugged each one.

They asked her very specific and personal questions which she answered convincingly. Their opinion was that no outsider could have had that information.

Subsequently the 'previous' family took her in a car and told her that a particular place was where Mukesh came from. She said, 'No, that is not it.' They did this twice until they took a particular turn in the road when Sonam volunteered, 'Yes, this is Batta.' She then began to give directions until they successfully reached the house where Mukesh had lived.

At first she was a bit confused as the house seemed different. She said that it used to be yellow. She was correct.

After Mukesh's death the parents added a floor and repainted the house. However she did recognise the gate and a relative of Mukesh, Meena, who was standing in the courtyard.

Inside the house Sonam saw a picture of Mukesh and said, 'That's me.' She also, unprompted, recognised a photograph of Mukesh's grandfather. Later she correctly recognised all sorts of relatives from photos.

After an hour or so, a very sceptical Meena was convinced that Sonam was who said she was.

On further questioning it became apparent that the families were very concerned and edgy about the army and didn't want to make waves.

During the first visit to Sonam the investigators were told that a man from a TV channel would also be there to interview her.

This is where the plot thickens.

The investigators thought it strange at the time that the man from the 'T.V. news channel' was only holding a small video camera, but paid little attention to that fact.

Subsequently the investigators tried to track down the man from the TV Channel, to no avail. That channel did not exist.

The fear now was that the T.V. man was from the army.

Because of this Sonam's parents did not want her questioned any more.

Mukesh died on the 27th July 2002

Sonam was born on the 12th May 2007

She spoke of a life as Mukesh from when she could barely speak properly.

She recognised places and people from the past without any hesitation. As already stated, the birth mark in the centre of her chest may or may not be relevant. The University of Virginia has, in the database of children who remember a previous life, a sizable number of children who display a birthmark which appears to correspond to the method of death of the previous personality. Indeed there can be more than one birthmark which appears to correspond. Sonam's experiences are typical of hundreds, if not thousands, of similar cases.

She recognised many more items than I can describe in the overview of this particular case.

It is interesting to note that Sonam's mother did not really believe in reincarnation before these events. She said, 'In fact I ignored Sonam's claims for a long time.'

Various people have offered Sonam money for her story, but she has flatly refused to take any; indicating that financial gain was not a motive for the somewhat reluctant claims.

Due to the nature of the information given by the young child and subsequent confirmations, fraud and misperception seem an unlikely explanation for these events.

In all these types of cases the investigators are *not* uneducated and gullible fools.

Dr Jim Tucker is a Professor of psychiatry and neurobehavioral sciences at the University of Virginia. In his latest book, *Return to Life*, he describes some extraordinary cases of children who remember a previous life. Jim himself has investigated and researched many of the intricate details in some of the cases.

One of the most extraordinary accounts tells of an American boy James who, from when he could speak, insisted that he had been a pilot during World War 2. From the age of two he began having terrible nightmares about a plane crash and he would say things like, 'little man can't get out' while screaming and shouting. When he was old enough to verbalise he said that he had been a pilot on the Ship, *Natoma* and he had been shot down in the Iwo Jima operation.

The amount of detail provided by this child subsequently enabled investigators to verify the majority of his statements, including his name and existence of the colleague that he had in 1944.

This makes a fascinating read and is in keeping with so many of the other 3000 cases on the database at the University of Virginia.

Chapter 10

OBSERVATIONS ON COMMON FEATURES WITHIN AUTHENTICATED CASES OF OSTENSIBLE OBSESSION, POSSESSION AND REINCARNATION.

It is well established in science that in trying to reach an understanding of a field of particular phenomena, a study of the similarities, or dissimilarities, among each of the individual cases is valuable if we are to try to attempt to formulate a theory or an understanding of it.

Let us apply this technique to the topic of ostensible reincarnation and/or obsession and possession.

Each of the cases listed in the following table was examined by eminent psychical researchers. Among these are Professor Ian Stevenson, Dr Hodgson (an avid sceptic originally), Dr Stevens, Professor A. Akolkar, Professor Pasricha, Dr Morton Prince, Professor Hyslop and Professor Erlendur Haraldsson.

It seems very clear to the author that "something" happens to a person before any of the aforementioned phenomena occurs. I will use the term that *the "lid" comes off* some part of that person's psyche before the phenomenon of change manifests.

Let us consider the following table which illustrates but a few examples of ostensible cases of obsession, possession and possible reincarnation.

Are these people merely playing some kind of psychic DVD (Downloading Veridical Data) from some sort of cosmic digital archive, or is something else going on?

Let us consider the following table.

Host: refers to the original personality displayed by a human body.

Incomer: refers to a personality manifesting through a body that had a different personality to begin with.

The small column that says yes or no refers to the question, 'Did the host exhibit any transient personality other than the one that settled as the eventual incomer?'

Host Age refers to when the host exhibited a change in personality or identity.

Incomer Death age refers to the age at which the incoming personality died.

C of death refers to host. Cause refers to the death condition of the incomer.

Host	Age	C of Death	Time between		Incomer	Death age	Cause
Jasbir LalJat (PP)	3.5 yrs	Small-pox	+/- hrs/ days	No transient	Sobha Ram	26 yrs	Fall after poisoning
Lurancy Vennum TP	14 yrs	Fits	13, 1/2 years	Yes	Mary Roff	19 yrs	Fits
Sumitra (PP)	20 yrs	Illness	2 mths	Yes	Shiva Tripathi	24 yrs	Possibly Murdered
Uttara (TP) Huddar	25 yrs	Extreme meditation	140 yrs	No	Sharada	23 yrs	Snake bite
Semih Tutusmus B.M. (R)?	2 yrs	When began speaking	2 yrs	No	SelimFesli	2 yrs	Shot in ear
Thompson (OB)	36 yrs		6 mths	No	Gifford	59 yrs aprox	aprox
Arigo (TP)	30 yrs	When he developed healing	Months	No	Dr Fritz	30 yrs aprox	War
Purnima (girl) B.M (R)?	2/3 yrs	When began speaking	5 yrs	No	Jinadasa (man)	36 yrs	Vehicle accident
Sonam (girl) (R)?	3 years	Began speaking	5 years	No	Murkesh (man)	19 yrs	Killed
Chatura Buddika B.M. (R)?	3 yrs	Began speaking	6 yrs	No	Dayananda	22 yrs	Bomb blast
James (R)?	2 yrs	When began speaking	44 years	no	James Huston	In his 20's	Shot down in the war.
Samuel Helander (R)?	Appx 2 yrs	When began speaking	Under 1 year	No	Pertti Haikio	18 yrs	Diabetes mellitus

(TP) = Temporary possession (PP) = permanent possession

OB = obsession B.M. = birth marks. (R)? = reincarnation

Sometimes it is noted that transient personalities manifest through a host before the final incomer 'settles'. These are usually of the recently deceased, who give their names and other details about themselves. Why should this be so?

Observations

The majority of incoming personalities have met a violent, early or unpleasant death.

Each incoming personality was reasonably young when they passed.

It would be impossible to discuss each of these cases in detail but, in the case of Sharada, which is one of temporary possession, the manifestations are still taking place perhaps once or twice a year.

What "allowed" any of the new personalities to present themselves? – Either temporarily or permanently. We have to ask ourselves the questions:

When did the lid come off the host's body?

Why did the lid come off the host's body?

What part of us, as human beings, normally holds the lid down?

If it is a file, an Akashic type record of a person, (quantum or otherwise) that displaces the old personality, why would a file do this? Why would a file have any impetus or intention to do this and what would be its motivation?

You will remember that in the case of Lurancy Vennum: while she was in an altered state due to having fits, two personalities made themselves known. One was an old woman called Katrina Hogan, the other a man called Willie Canning. Both were very recently deceased. Again I ask why should this be so? With Sumitra the transients identified themselves as a woman from Sharif Pura, who had drowned herself in a well, and a man from a different Indian State.

Why are the transient personalities those of the recently deceased?

Why did the final personalities displace the recently deceased ones?

Is it a matter of need, will power or some other kind of strength?

(Musical bodies?); when the music stops jump into the empty chair?

If it is all role-playing and imagination on the part of the hosts, why is it that the new personalities who remained did actually exist and nearly all met untimely deaths?

If a person was downloading another person's file from some type of Akashic record then surely, by chance, a good percentage of them would be from people who lived full and happy lives. This does not seem to be the case, which should give us even more food for thought.

What is to be made of all of this is up to the individual, but to anyone of open mind it must, at least, give one pause and food for thought.

The author wonders that, if similar circumstances could occur again in each individual case, would the outcome be of a similar nature?

How many other cases do we not know about?

As it would be impossible to go through every case on the above chart, I provide sources for your further reading for those who wish to read more on P. 170.

Chapter 11

A MEDLEY OF PHENOMENA

Jenny

A few years ago, before the proliferation of mobile phones, a lady arranged to meet me to discuss unusual experiences that she had been having, as she was mystified by some of them. This lady had been reading books about out-of-body experience, hereafter referred to as OBE, and how to achieve them. I cannot recommend that anyone should try this on their own.

Her son had moved to South Africa with his wife and new baby. My lady, let's call her Jenny, had seen this baby boy when newly born but not during the last two and a half years. As she was missing him and curious to know what he looked like she thought, in her wisdom, that she would try the techniques that she had read about in books and achieve an OBE to South Africa to see her grandchild. Foolishly she did this one night and found herself in black space looking down on a vague light, far, far away in the distance; she was terrified and glad when, quote, she "wooshed" (her words) back into her body.

Undaunted, she tried again another night. When she had been out in South Africa two and a half years previously she had obviously been in her son's home; as part of the technique used to travel out of body she had to visualise her son's living room and concentrate on it. Jenny found herself in that living room, but it was empty of furniture and anything else. She was puzzled for a time then "wooshed" back into her body again. Now any of you who have sons living away from home will relate to the fact that they are wonderful communicators. (Joke). The next day she telephoned him at his work to discover that he had moved home and therefore the house that she had "visited" the night before would have been empty at the time of her OBE escapade. Needless to say she did not tell her son of the attempt. Yet again undaunted, she knew from her last visit where, in South Africa, his wife's parents lived, as she had visited their home when she was there; so Jenny was off again to the aforesaid house. She found herself in a position around the ceiling of the living room where she "saw" her son's father-in-law sitting in a chair, reading a paper. He looked up slowly, his face turned white, and he yelled, "You can't touch me I'm a Christian." Jenny was amazed as it appeared that the man could also see her. Actually she found that experience quite amusing. Once again she "wooshed" back into her body.

After making further inquiry and having now established the location of the son's *new* home, she built a picture in her mind regarding the map references and she tried again. This time she found herself in a home that she did not know, she observed the style and colours of the lounge suite, the curtains and other furnishings before "wooshing" back again. The next day she wrote to her son and asked him to write and describe, among other things, his lounge suite. The descriptions matched the room that she "saw." She was still not convinced and, getting cocky now, she tried again and found herself at the edge of a park looking at some children playing; she saw one little boy and just knew that it was her grandson. That child looked up and pointed to Jenny, tugging at his mother's skirt, and said, "look at lady" and he smiled at Jenny. The mother said no, no dear there's no one there. It was time for Jenny to 'woosh" again.

She and I had a long series of conversations, during which I asked if anyone else in the family had ever had a strange experience of any kind and I was surprised by her answers.

During the investigation of spontaneous cases, one of the standard questions is to inquire into to family background regarding paranormal experiences. Very often there is nothing to report, but we always ask.

Jenny was married with two children, a boy and a girl, with twelve years difference in age between them, the boy being older. When the boy was under five years of age and playing happily on the lounge floor of their home with his toys, while Jenny and husband were sitting on armchairs at either side of the fireplace reading newspapers, Jenny said to her husband, "Will I read your horoscope, you're Leo aren't you?" Before he could reply the son piped up, while still playing with his toys, "No, dad's a Libra and mum's a Leo."

Jenny looked at him and said, "No dear, dad's a Leo and I'm an Aries, you are getting mixed up. With a tone of great impatience he repeated his first statement and said, "I don't mean you.... I mean the Mummy and Daddy I had before!".... with the inflection indicating "How can you be so stupid, you know what I mean."

The parents did not say anything at that time but later on, in private, Jenny asked him in a gentle way what he meant about another mum and dad. He told her that his last father was an engineer and mummy was a beautiful lady with a big dress down to the floor; he had seven brothers and sisters and they had two sons called Matthew. Jenny said, "You couldn't have had two Matthews in the one family." Without turning a hair he replied, "Yes we did, one baby boy was born and named Matthew but he died. Later on mummy had another boy and she called him Matthew too."

He volunteered the fact that he had a sister Susan who died with a lot of spots on her face. Jenny asked him, "What happened to you?" to be told that he had a sore head and lay down and the next thing he knew he was here with Jenny. She told me that he sounded so disappointed. The matter was never mentioned again. Several months later husband and wife were going out to a special occasion that required semi-formal dress. When Jenny came down the stairs in her home, dressed for the evening out, the son looked up briefly from his toys, gave a huge smile and said, "Beautiful lady just like my mummy."

Father cringed, as he did not like the mention of anything like this.

Another few months later, after saying his prayers at bedtime, the son imparted information to Jenny to the effect that sometimes a man wearing a long dress and sandals appeared at the foot of his bed and wanted him to go with him. This was worrying and she told him that he must not go, to which he readily agreed. About a month later he said that the man had gone, at which she breathed a sigh of relief but as a curiosity, and she does not know why she asked, she asked him HOW (i.e. by what means) the man wanted him to go. He replied that the man wanted him to go up on a ladder.

No more questions were asked and that seemed to be the end of the events.

When her daughter, who was twelve years younger than her brother, was about four years of age and playing about the house with her toys, she suddenly volunteered the following information to Jenny, "You know I didn't want to come here." Jenny looked at her blankly and said, "What do you mean, you are at home." The child replied, "No I mean here, I was somewhere nice with a lot of people and someone said to me that a man 'down there' needs a wee girl and that is going to be you, and in some way I could see Daddy." For want of anything else to say Jenny said, "How did you get here?" The reply was, "I came down on a ladder."

Now remembering that there is twelve years difference in the children's ages, I feel that it is very unlikely that a sixteen year old boy and a four year old girl would have any collusion in this matter.

As far as Jenny is concerned, she finds it amusing, although a bit offended, that she has two children who did not seem to appear to want to be with her, as though she was a kind of spiritual second best.

I must now state again that I could not advise anyone to try to induce an out-of-body experience, although others may disagree with me.

However, out-of-body experiences which occur "naturally" seem to have a different quality.

David

A child known to me for many years, from a family of good character, had an OBE, bordering on a near-death experience (NDE) around the age of seven. The child was asthmatic and at this time had a bad cold. One evening his father looked into the bedroom to check that he was all right and found that he did not appear to be breathing. The parents rushed him to hospital after the mother, who had medical training, managed to start him breathing again. The hospital kept him in overnight for observation and he was discharged the next day.

Every night before going into bed the mother always said prayers with him; the usual "God bless mummy, God bless daddy." A few days after the hospital event, before prayers started, the child turned to his mother and said, "Do you think I'll go to see God again tonight?"

She said words to the effect that she did not know that he had seen God before. His reply was, "You know, the night I was taken to hospital!" Displaying her ignorance she asked him to tell her about it, saying that she had just forgotten. The child described going up a beautiful tunnel of light which was so bright, but it didn't hurt his eyes; it was so peaceful and he could hear birds singing, there was lovely music which he had never heard before, there were flowers with colours he had never seen before and a wonderful scent of perfume everywhere. As he quite happily progressed up the tunnel he saw a lady in front of him who held her hand up and said, "No David, go back to mummy, it's not time for you to come any further." My friend did not really know how to respond but muttered something suitable and left it at that.

Months later, at the boy's grandmother's house, the child was playing with toys around the house while mum and grandmother were looking through old photographs, minding their own business as it were, when the boy skipped passed them and pointed to a picture and said, "That's her." The two women looked at him, wondering what he was talking about and asked what he meant. He replied, "That's the lady who told me to come back to mummy."

The picture was of the child's great-grandmother, whom he had never met and incidentally she does not look like his grandmother in any way at all.

Knowing the credibility of the family concerned, I would not doubt their statements.

Life Changing

A few years ago there were a couple of television appearances by an ex wing commander, a man of the highest calibre, who gave an account of his unforgettable out of body and near-death experience. I was involved in another part of one of those programmes. No one who saw these programmes could doubt his sincerity and the profound effect that the events had on him. It changed his life, and he freely admitted that he did not want to "come back" as the experience was one of such love and understanding, beauty, euphoria and joy, but the thought which brought him back was that he had to tell his loved ones of the joy which lies ahead of them and to tell them that after his experience, there is nothing to fear in dying.

He spoke of leaving his body and going through a kind of tunnel of vibrant light, being wrapped in that light, which produced in him such a feeling of joy and beauty and most of all an overwhelming feeling of being loved, the kind of feeling that tells you that you are truly loved and cherished no matter what happens. He described being in what seemed like a very large room, but it had no ceiling and seemed to go on forever. He then met "people" and had conversations with them, and, as he put it, suddenly he "knew" everything, everything made sense, his life, the world, and all related matters showed their purpose, fell into place and the reasons behind events became clear. He said that it was so simple that a child could understand it.

He has never forgotten one detail of those events, even after many years, which as I will continue to reiterate, is always an indicator in any form of paranormal activity as to its veracity. There was no reason in the gentleman's life at this time for him to be stressed; in fact just the opposite was true. He was very content and happy having found a lovely new wife; therefore the sceptics cannot say that he was looking for an escape from life. We are not looking at a case of oxygen deprivation causing strange effects to the brain as this man, more than others, was in a better position to know, having actually experienced oxygen starvation many years previously while in wartime action.

He testifies that the two incidents bore no relation to each other in any way at all, as with oxygen deprivation the mind becomes cloudy and confused, whereas with the near-death experience the clarity of mind is beyond description, both during the experience and on returning to what we call consciousness. The experience was so beautiful that he did not want to come back, until he remembered about his new wife and forced himself back to tell her that there was nothing to fear in dying.

It is worth mentioning here, yet again, that anyone who has a genuine paranormal experience never forgets it, no matter how long ago it occurred. Every facet of that experience is remembered with crystal clarity; not a moment is forgotten.

Dr Eben Alexander

This gentleman is an esteemed American neurosurgeon, who had no previous interest in paranormal events. In 2010 he contracted viral meningitis in the cortex of his brain. This is not a good scenario and it should have been fatal. During his time in critical care in hospital he had a near-death experience which changed his outlook on life and death. His experience resulted in his writing a book called *Proof of Heaven*. Because of his knowledge and expertise in the workings of the brain, he lays out quite clearly the impossibility of his experiences actually coming from, or through, his physical brain. This is an expert's opinion and he really does know what he is talking about.

These examples are but part of an enormous collection of such accounts, which would lead a sensible person to the conclusion that this subject must be taken seriously. Between out of body and near-death experiences we surely have enough evidence to conclude that it is possible for the consciousness of a human being to "leave his /her body" for a period of time.

Closer to The Light is one of the many good books on this topic. It is by Dr Melvin Morse, a hospital doctor, who started out as a complete sceptic and controlled a very large scientific study of patients who reported a near-death experience. Certain criteria were followed; for example, any people on any medication which might affect their judgement were omitted from the statistics.

Over a fairly long period of time, data was gathered in and people interviewed. A number of fully qualified medical doctors were involved in this venture.

The resulting book is most interesting, with many cases fitting the parameters already discussed in this chapter.

The British neuroscientist Dr Peter Fenwick and his wife Elizabeth are also at the forefront of this work, cooperating with nurses and doctors in gathering data on the N.D.E.

It is interesting to note that near-death experiences are very similar throughout the world. Due to different cultures the interpretation of the 'glowing figure' who meets them can be expressed as Jesus, Moses, Abraham, etc. dependent on the background of the person having the experience. In one of Morse's books a little boy speaks of meeting the 'crystal clown.' at the end of the tunnel. I thought that was lovely.

There is almost an embarrassment of books on the near-death experience, one of the latest being by Dr Penny Sartori, *The Wisdom of Near-Death Experiences*. This is not a bad thing and it shows that these experiences are much more common than we think and, as previously said, there are so many interesting and possibly meaningful common factors.

There are a few accounts of people who have a negative near-death experience. Because of this, in the majority of these cases, the person changes his/her lifestyle after returning to this life and normal consciousness, as they don't want to go back to that negative place when their time does come.

Chapter 12

RESISTANCE TO ACCEPTING PARANORMAL PHENOMENA

The greatest obstacle to people's acceptance of the reality of paranormal events is not the lack of evidence that is available but the firmly entrenched belief that such events are impossible. They think that such things cannot happen, so they do not happen and those who say they do are gullible, careless, incompetent or foolish, the victims of clever fraudsters or even fraudulent themselves. Indeed many eminent psychical researchers, even when presented with convincing evidence from personal experiences that paranormal events occur, have drawn attention to this phenomenon and have, much to their dismay, discovered it in themselves. Professor Charles Richet, world-renowned physiologist and Nobel Laureate, a keen, sceptical and long-term researcher into alleged psychic phenomena, wrote after his carefully conducted series of tests of Eusapia Palladino, the famous - some would say notorious - physical medium:

> But at this point a remarkable psychological phenomenon made itself
> felt; a phenomenon deserving of all your attention. Observe that we

99

are now dealing with observed facts which are nevertheless absurd; which are in contradiction with facts of daily observation; which are denied not by science only, but by the whole of humanity - facts which are rapid and fugitive, which take place in semi-darkness, and almost by surprise; with no proof except the testimony of our senses, which we know to be often fallible. After we have witnessed such facts, everything concurs to make us doubt them. Now, at the moment when these facts take place they seem to us certain, and we are willing to proclaim them openly; but when we return to ourselves, when we feel the irresistible influence of our environment, when our friends all laugh at our credulity – then we are almost disarmed, and we began to doubt. May it not all have been an illusion? May I not have been grossly deceived? ... And then, as the moment of the experiment becomes more remote, that experiment, which once seemed so conclusive gets to seem more and more uncertain, and we end by letting ourselves be persuaded that we have been the victims of a trick.

Again the Hon. Everard Fielding, who was a member of the magic circle, one of the most cautious investigators of the paranormal, said:

The effect of all this on my mind was singular; I appeared to lose touch with actualities. Once admit the possibility of such things and the mere fact of investigating them implied such an admission – where could one stop? I wrote at the time that I gradually began to feel that if a man told me that the statue of the Albert Memorial had called in to tea I should have to admit that the question to be solved would not be the sanity of the narrator but the evidence for the fact.

The philosopher Emmanuel Kant was well aware of the effect on himself on hearing the testimony of many respected witnesses who claimed to have been present when the famous scientist, engineer and psychic Emmanuel Swedenborg gave information about events and people that he could have had no means of obtaining in any normal manner.

In 1759 Swedenborg was one of sixteen guests at dinner at the Gothenburg Mansion. It was noticed that about six o'clock in the evening he became alarmed. He informed the company that a fire had broken out in Stockholm – about three hundred miles away. At intervals thereafter he told the guests of the progress of the conflagration, commenting on whose house had now been consumed by the fire. Later still in

the evening he jumped up exclaiming, "God be praised! It has been put out just a few houses from mine."

Swedenborg also gave a detailed account of the disaster to the Governor two days before messengers arrived with reports relating how the fire had indeed developed exactly according to the 'eye-witness bulletins'. Swedenborg was correct in the details that he had given the guests of the fire's progress. Immanuel Kant investigated this event, noted that the guests were reliable and creditable witnesses, and thereafter admitted that he himself had been much disturbed by it by finding himself unable to believe or disbelieve in it. In such a worrying mental situation the person in that disturbed frame of mind often ends up clinging to his former belief system by gradually dismissing from his mind the contradictory testimony that threatens his confidence in the stability of his world. Kant was suffering the unpleasant experience of cognitive dissonance. The *Britannica Concise Encyclopaedia* defines cognitive dissonance as: "Mental conflict that occurs when beliefs or assumptions are contradicted by new information." Also defined as, "A mismatch between what is perceived and what 'is'."

There are many more occasions where it would appear that Swedenborg, in his post-natural philosopher mode, was clairvoyant, clairaudient and even precognitive. He continued to live his strange life, publishing his careful, scientific and detailed descriptions of the new realms, their inhabitants and their moral laws. He now seemed able to enter, observe and study these realms at will, yet he still travelled extensively in the physical world and still demonstrated to his friends that he had lost nothing of his scientific intelligence. This last phase of his life lasted almost thirty years. Indeed his mind remained clear until his death at the age of eighty-four in London, England, a death whose date he had predicted with complete equanimity. When he learned that the Wesleys, the great evangelists, wished to meet him in April or May he wrote back that it would be too late for by then he would have passed on. It is on record that Swedenborg only paid his rent up until the end of March. Having thanked his landlady for her services, he retired upstairs to his room where he died on March 29, 1772.

I have no clear understanding of what happened to Swedenborg following his intention to research deeply into the human soul. Nevertheless he appeared to achieve much in a short period of time. Having progressed from his productive, wide-ranging scientific and engineering researches within the natural, inanimate world to attention to botany, biology and human anatomy, particularly the structure and function of the brain, he somehow by his new activities now gained access into spiritual realms, remaining sane and even objective in his exploration of them; his conclusions and teachings thereafter being built with important and distinctly radical differences upon the religious, protestant foundation that he had been exposed to in his youth.

The facts about this remarkable man, vouched for by the innumerable people of good reputation who witnessed them, challenge us to take seriously the possibility that the mind has hidden dimensions and extensions beyond the confines of the brain. Unless we can find some flaw in all the witnesses' testimony we have to face the uneasiness that many people have felt exactly the same when they first come across the possibility that strange things, inexplicable by the accepted and tested laws of science, can actually happen.

In science, a paradigm is essentially a belief system of what is possible in nature; it can take form when a long era of successful advances in science seems to complete our state of knowledge and understanding of an important field of natural phenomena. The word paradigm is defined as, 'A set of assumptions, concepts, values and practices that constitutes a way of viewing reality for the community that shares them, especially in an intellectual discipline.'

One such paradigm arose from the pioneering work of Isaac Newton in the 17th century from his work in celestial mechanics, which provided the reasons why stars, planets and moons orbited as they did. Two centuries later a second paradigm stemmed from the work of Faraday and Clerk Maxwell on electromagnetism and light. A third paradigm on atomic physics issued from the early discoveries of J. J. Thomson, Lord Rutherford and Lord Rayleigh. Each earlier paradigm, in general, has resisted the discoveries of later scientists as if they were a threat to its existence. Indeed they are, almost as if the earlier species is a species threatened by an unforeseen environmental change. In Darwinian terms, if the paradigm does not evolve it is doomed to extinction. Professor Bernard Carr, a former SPR President and a renowned physicist has remarked in *Worlds apart*;

> Can psychical research bridge the gulf between matter and mind, during the [paradigm] crisis, a variety of new theories will be advanced. The upholders of the old paradigm will try to resist these but eventually they die off and the new paradigm takes hold. If it is lucky, however, the old paradigm may indeed still be useful in its own way. The complete success of the Cassini-Huyghens space mission to Saturn and its

moons was not only a triumph for modern space flight, science and technology but was also based on Newton's Law of Gravitation and the three Laws of Motion.

Quotes regarding avid scepticism about the paranormal.

Sociologists Harry Collins and Trevor Pinch[12] made a study of the way in which parapsychology has been treated by its critics in the main scientific journals. They found straight forward statements of prejudice; pseudo-philosophic arguments to the effect that parapsychology ought to be rejected simply because it conflicts with accepted knowledge; accusations of fraud without any evidence to support them; attempts to discredit scientific parapsychology by association with cult and fringe activities, and emotional dismissals based only on grounds that the consequences of its acceptance would be too horrible to contemplate. They concluded that the ordinary standards and procedures of scientific debate were being seriously violated. This fear, in the minds of some sceptics, seems to stem from a perceived threat to the structure of science.

> However, Henry Margenau, physicist, has shown that it is impossible to identify a single scientific law actually threatened by the reality of paranormal phenomena. He points out that the Law of Conservation of Energy and Momentum has already been broken by discoveries in quantum physics, which also deal with non-locality or action at a distance; and that nothing in parapsychological discoveries contradicts either the Second Law of Thermodynamics or the Principle of Causality. The only contradictions that seem to exist are with our culturally accepted view of reality based on such laws.[13]

Psychologist, Charles Tart, University of California, suggests that the emotional nature of the debate might be due to the fact that discoveries in parapsychology offer a more personal kind of threat which operates through unconscious fears of the subject. This is clearly not the whole answer, but I find such psychological explanations very persuasive; science is not so much a body of undisputed fact as a set of perceptions about facts that are, on the whole, very useful, but occasionally harden

---

[12] Collins and Pinch "The construction of the paranormal"

[13] Lawrence Le Shan *From Newton to ESP*

into dogma. Normal science is guided by a substantive set of beliefs held, both consciously and unconsciously by the scientific community. And anything that starts out by defining itself from the beginning as paranormal is likely to be more comfortably dismissed as irrelevant.

So you see, everyone, that we are really "up against it". A good scientist should go where the evidence leads, but stubborn ingrained teachings can sometimes make this extremely difficult for us all.

Chapter 13

MEDIUMSHIP

As opposed to séances producing materialisations, where physical mediums come into play, there were, and are, many good mediums simply called mental mediums. (No jokes please.) Most of the genuine trance (mental) mediums studied by psychical researchers have also exhibited so-called controls who act as masters of ceremonies in transmitting information to a sitter. These controls may also 'step aside' on occasion, allowing the communicator to control the medium's organism and converse directly with a sitter. The communicator's response in such a conversation may be made by automatic script or speech. It is said that part of the duties of a control is to act as a kind of gate-keeper and protect the medium's body from any unwanted intruders from 'the other side' trying to gate-crash the proceedings. Some benign intruders appear to be allowed through and they may give information totally unknown to sitters, information that sometimes can be verified only after a long subsequent investigation. As already stated, a successful intruder is often referred to as a 'drop-in' communicator and some psychical researchers, including myself, are of the opinion that they provide not only strong evidence of the essentially paranormal content of genuine mediumship, but also make it difficult to avoid considering survival of death of some sort as the most parsimonious explanation for the phenomenon.

Although many of the following accounts are historical, they must *not* be forgotten since they are as relevant today as they were in their time. In other words there is no best before or sell-by date on them.

Among the great mediums who had controls were Mrs Piper, Mrs Leonard, Mrs Garrett and Miss Geraldine Cummins. Dr Phinuit, Mrs Piper's control, could not be taken at face value. He had a distinct personality, irascible and touchy, and claimed to be the spirit of an old French medical man yet none of the details of his C.V. were borne out by research. Phinuit would act in the usual manner of a master of ceremonies, ostensibly performing as an intermediary between the sitters and the spirits of the deceased, who were often relatives of the sitters who appeared anxious to convince the sitters that they had survived death. Sometimes Phinuit was on top form, describing in accurate terms the deceased relatives of the sitters and relaying their purported statements plus a host of relevant facts that Mrs Piper could not have learned about in any conceivable normal way.

But Dr Phinuit could fall down. The investigators recognised that on occasion he could employ tricks, fishing to obtain information from the sitters. Dr Richard Hodgson, who made a life study of Mrs Piper's mediumship remarked that he had been at sittings where Phinuit has displayed such pattering and equivocation, and such a lack of lucidity, that I believe had these been my only experiences with him I should have without any hesitation have condemned Mrs Piper as an imposter.' Phinuit himself confessed, 'Sometimes when I come here, do you know, actually it is hard work for me to get control of the medium. Sometimes I think I am almost like the medium, and sometimes not at all. Then [when the control is incomplete] I am weak and confused.

Hodgson also noticed that when Phinuit was having difficulty in getting names or other data that a sitter presumably had in the forefront of their mind he would change the subject and often be successful when the sitter was no longer thinking consciously about it. It was as if the desire from the sitter was actually a hindrance.

A visit by Mrs Piper to England in 1889 produced fresh evidence of her ability in trance to acquire, in a paranormal fashion, obscure pieces of information. Both Sir Oliver Lodge and Frederic Myers became totally convinced that these powers existed. In particular Lodge brought to her over forty people, all strangers to her. The information that she, or rather her control Dr Phinuit, provided in many cases was shown on subsequent inquiry to be correct, even when the sitter had no conscious recollection or knowledge at the time that it was. In his report

Lodge also discussed the way in which Dr Phinuit, seemingly at times baffled by a lack of information, would 'fish' skilfully for clues among the sitters; at other times, however, the flow of facts would come easily and impressively.

One morning Lodge unexpectedly received a gold watch from one of his uncles. He handed it to Mrs Piper when she was in trance. Dr Phinuit told him that the watch had belonged to another of Lodge's uncles. He then described episodes and adventures of the uncles when they were boys. Lodge could neither confirm nor deny these alleged events. When he consulted his uncle he found that he had forgotten most of the details. Only when they got in touch with yet another uncle was the information confirmed.

By 1896, Dr Hodgson, formerly very suspicious of these matters, who began from an attitude of extreme scepticism, witnessed a remarkable development in Mrs Piper's mediumship. On March 12, 1892, a sitter had taken several test articles to Mrs Piper, among them a ring that had belonged to an Annie D. Hodgson comments,

> Phinuit made references to this lady, giving the name Annie, and just before the close of the sitting Mrs Piper's right hand moved slowly up until it was over the top of her head. The arm seemed to become rigidly fixed in its position, as though spasmodically contracted, but the hand trembled very rapidly. Phinuit exclaimed several times, "She's taken my hand away", and added, "she wants to write". I put a pencil between the [medium's] fingers, and placed a block-book on the head under the pencil. No writing came until, obeying Phinuit's order to "hold the hand", I grasped the hand very firmly at its junction with the wrist and so stopped its trembling or vibrating. It then wrote, "I am Annie D- [surname correctly given]... I am not dead... I am not dead but living. . . . I am not dead. . . world. . .goodbye. . . I am Annie D-". The hold on the pencil then relaxed, and Phinuit began to murmur, "Give me my hand back, give me my hand back." The arm, however, remained in its contracted position for a short time, but finally, as though with much difficulty, and slowly, it moved down to the side and Phinuit appeared to regain control over it.

This strange new automatic writing facility developed rapidly, but the writing did not necessarily silence Phinuit. On many occasions, while Phinuit would be conversing audibly with one sitter, the hand would be writing answers to questions by another sitter so that, by this means, two entirely different discourses would be proceeding independently of one another involving two ostensibly different entities and two sitters.

Now that is impressive!

At one sitting, Hodgson reported,

> where a lady was engaged in a profoundly personal conversation with Phinuit concerning her relations, and where I was present to assist, knowing the lady and her family very intimately, the hand was seized very quietly and, as it were, surreptitiously, and wrote a very personal communication to myself, purporting to come from a deceased friend of mine, and having no relation whatsoever to the sitter; precisely as if a caller should enter a room where two strangers to him were conversing, but a friend of his also present, and whisper a special message into the ear of the friend without disturbing the conversation.

In the case of the medium Mrs Leonard her control, Feda, claimed to be a young girl who had been a Hindu ancestress of Mrs Leonard, in fact Mrs Leonard's own great-great-grandmother. She said she had been raised by a Scottish family until the age of thirteen, and had then married an Englishman, William Hamilton, dying a year later in childbirth in 1800. Mrs Leonard recalled that her mother had told her about this Hindu ancestress. She remained Mrs Leonard's control for more than forty years of her career as a medium.

Sitters generally got an impression of Feda as a usually happy childlike girl with a high-pitched voice and an often mischievous sense of humour, who wanted to do her best to help. On occasion she told sitters that she was learning and progressing through controlling Mrs Leonard and helping to link up people on earth with the ones they loved on the other side. She could become uncertain or wary if she did not quite know what to make of some sitters or communicators and at times could be disapproving of them - even of Mrs Leonard herself. Over the years, Feda seemed to mature somewhat though still retained much of her childlike nature; some of her mispronunciations of words remained, together with grammatical errors and seeming misunderstanding of certain meanings of specific words.

An interesting feature of the mediumship was the occasional phenomenon of the sitters hearing another direct voice, quite different from Feda's, which sometimes corrected Feda's errors. Feda sometimes argued with this direct voice, which appeared to come from a different part of the room. Professor C.D. Broad, the eminent Cambridge philosopher, was among the psychical researchers who studied Mrs Leonard's mediumship. Once, while delivering a lecture on psychical research, he sent a frisson of surprise around his audience by looking up from his notes and stating that he had heard the direct voice *himself*.

Again, the problem of Feda's real nature remains. Broad and others tended to support the idea that the control was no more than a type of secondary personality of the medium.

To a large extent, the same questions may be asked about Mrs Garrett's control Uvani and Miss Cummins' control Astor. These controls also stayed with their mediums for many years, claiming to be independent spirits. Miss Cummins herself, showing a true Irish spirit of independence, expressed her dislike for the word 'control', maintaining that Astor never controlled her but likened her to Socrates' "Daemon" who advised him.

In this matter the work of the respected Irish medium Geraldine Cummins, who was studied for many years by psychical researchers, is not irrelevant. Much of the material received by Miss Cummins was by automatic writing, with script being written at tremendous speed. In an hour and a half she might write over 2000 words. It was the task of a helper, when a sheet of paper was filled with script, to remove it and replace it by a fresh sheet. Over the years many different kinds of psychic tests were carried out on Miss Cummins; experiments in precognition, psychometry and psychical medical diagnosis in collaboration with Dr Connell, a Fellow of the Royal College of Physicians, Ireland. She also gave sittings with Miss Gibbes, the lady who had encouraged Miss Cummins in her work, for those whom Miss Gibbes felt were in real need of help. Geraldine continued this work after Miss Gibbes's death. In her psychic work she too on occasion also had 'drop-in' communicators who gate crashed the sittings. I stress again, at risk of boring you, that these 'drop-in' cases are instructive and extremely difficult to fit into the super-ESP theory which supposes that a medium almost instantaneously trawls through living people's minds or brains or even through newspapers and other documents to find facts or memories of a dead person that can be woven into a passable presentation of that person.

In one of her 'drop-in' cases, scripts were received from a deceased Dr Tomlin for a Mrs Wilson (pseudonym) and were posted to her.

In them Dr Tomlin gave names and facts about himself, his wife and daughter. A number of the facts were unknown to Mrs Wilson who had them subsequently verified by Dr Tomlin's daughter. The daughter confirmed that her life as given in the scripts was accurately described and also that not only had she never met or heard of Miss Cummins but also knew no-one acquainted with Miss Cummins except Mrs Wilson. Miss Cummins wrote of this case,

> According to one anti-survival theory, Dr Tomlin was extinct as an individual, and I was merely stealing his neatly tabulated memories from an alleged Common Unconscious. But how then in these scripts did this static Great Memory demonstrate a very active survival in Tomlin's case, showing his characteristic jealousy of his daughter's husband and exhibiting in unscrupulous action an agitated mind tormented by hatred and frustration?'

> 'This case and others show that when an intruding stranger is driven by a powerful emotion of love, jealousy or hatred he appears to be able, through its power, to overcome all difficulties of transmission and to be able to convey verifiable facts, as did Tomlin. His active, hate-driven mind endeavoured with threats to break up the happy marriage of a living couple. We do not seem to have static existence in the Hereafter, but continue our progress either for evil or for good. I felt extremely repelled by the unpleasant personality of Dr Tomlin and I stopped his later attempts to write through me.

One of the many cases investigated by Miss Gibbes concerned scripts purporting to come from the deceased wife of a Mr Carter, along with her sister Miss Primrose and a mutual friend of theirs, a Mr Tom Moore. In all, the scripts extended in time to ten sittings and contained not only evidence relating to their survival, in a manner characteristic of their different personalities, but also contained intimate details of family affairs connected with Mr and Mrs Carter. When Mr Carter received the communications he marvelled at them stating that each personality was unmistakable, but ordered them to be destroyed for he did not want such private matters to be found after his death. Mr Tom Moore's widow also testified that the writings ostensibly from her dead husband were exactly like him in style and declared her conviction that her husband had communicated. Miss Gibbes stated that although Miss Cummins had never seen any one of these communicators in life, she 'reproduced their different characteristics, their style of speech and phraseology, and references to family feuds and differences which had occurred before she was born.'

The Cross Correspondences

The cross correspondences were a kind of mediumship jigsaw puzzle. The information given through different mediums from different countries only really made sense when the information was combined and collated. Many of the allusions and inferences given by separate mediums were of classical origins and required well educated informed minds to interpret the information.

The Cross-Correspondences were, and are, so complicated that it is difficult to grasp the intricacies of them, especially in our present age when hardly anyone has a literary or classical education at all comparable with Myers, Verrall and Butcher, et al. Some of the information gathered, allusions, themes and puzzles were delivered over a period of years. Let us look at one particular case.

The Lethe Case

This example shows why the investigators took the Cross-Correspondences very seriously indeed. It is the Lethe Case (PSPR, volumes 24 and 25). Although not strictly part of the Cross-Correspondences, it is worth relating here for several reasons, and not merely because it is one of the classics of psychical research. Not only was it one of the reasons why Mrs Willett was recognised by the investigators as an outstanding medium, but it also exemplified the sort of case that persuaded the generally sceptical researchers to acknowledge the very tenuous basis on which any explanation other than one presuming on the active participation of a discarnate intelligence could be advanced. Moreover, it centred on the evidentiality of the deceased Frederic Myers whose messages were being channelled, so it was claimed, through two mediums thousands of miles apart, and it represents aspects of Myer's learning and character without plunging the reader into the labyrinthine maze of so many of the cross-correspondence puzzles.

In March, 1908, George Dorr, a Vice-President of the ASPR, was conducting a long series of sittings with the American medium Mrs Piper. At that time not only was the 'Hodgson' entity still communicating through her but also a person claiming to be Frederic Myers. Sometimes both entities were ostensibly 'present' at the same time so that a three-cornered 'conversation' between sitter, 'Myers' and 'Hodgson' would take place. Dorr decided to invite the Myers entity to say through voice or pen what the word 'Lethe' suggested to him.

Mrs Piper was ignorant of the Classics, but responded by producing in trance a string of references, almost all of them drawn from Ovid's *Metamorphoses*. When the results, which greatly impressed Dorr, were later brought to the attention of Sir Oliver Lodge in London, he decided, some six months later, to pose the *same* question to Mrs Willett in England, through whom the same personality claimed to be speaking. Lodge took the precaution of putting the question in a sealed envelope, to be opened only when the medium was satisfied that the question could be put to Myers (w) ['Myers' communicating through Mrs Willett]. The medium received the sealed envelope on September 30, 1909. When it was opened and the question in it put to Myers (w), the response contained another similar stream of accurate names and places relating to Lethe, but this time all drawn from references appearing in Virgil's *Aeneid*. Lodge had not expected the responses to be identical, if only because it was generally accepted that a medium's mind often has a contaminating or distorting effect on the thoughts or words transmitted. He was surprised, however, at the large number of accurate references, nearly all of them drawn from a different classical source, which displayed sufficient overlap with the earlier Piper communication to fortify the belief that the same intelligence must have been responsible.

The Willett script showed clearly that her communicator was well aware of what had been transmitted by 'Myers' via Piper [Myers (p)] in the USA. Not only did he, or it, get the bemused Mrs Willett to scribble the name "Dorr" several times, but he inserted a quotation which, he said, was "nothing of the normal intelligence of my machine", i.e. Mrs Willett. The quotation referred to a "door to which I found no key and Haggi Babba" [Ali Baba]. To ram home the allusion, there followed a reference to Open Sesame. (As in open the 'dorr'.) As for references to Lethe, the name of the river which flows past the fields of Elysium and from which the newly dead, if destined to return to earth, must first wash away their earthly sins and memories by drinking its purifying waters, Myers (w) quoted directly from the Sixth Book of the *Aeneid*: "The will again to live. The will again to live the River of Forgetfulness". This quotation is also to be found in Myers' own essay on Virgil (*Classical Essays*, p.174), and was incorporated in his poem, *The Passing of Youth*. This could hardly be coincidental, because the first response which Myers (p) had earlier given through Piper to the same question was "Do you refer to one of my poems?"

To ensure that the earthly investigators could not ascribe this to Mrs Willett's subliminal recollection of a Myers poem she might once have read, the Willett script was scattered with arcane but accurate references to the Lethe theme. *In Valle Reducta* (a sheltered vale) is the opening phrase of Virgil's description of the Lethe in the *Aeneid*, and there follow references by Myers (w) to bees and lilies, mainly in the form of Latin quotations. Less direct, but more characteristic of Myers, are his references to the Doves and the Golden Bough amid the Shadows, relating to the branch which Aeneas had to obtain before he could enter the infernal regions in order to arrive at the river of Lethe.

Subsequent scripts show the Myers (w) source overflowing with allusions inspired with the Lethe theme. Among these was mention of "Darien, a peak in Darien", a clear reference to Keat's sonnet describing Cortez's vision of the Pacific Ocean from a peak in Darien. This phrase had been occasionally employed by the S.P.R. founders to signify cases where dying persons seemed to catch glimpses of another world. In the deluge of information showered on the bewildered Mrs Willett by the author of her automatic scripts, no effort is spared to link the Lethe theme with Myer's own works and beliefs. However, whereas the Lethe passage in Virgil may readily be taken to indicate that souls prepare themselves for re-birth once all mundane memory had been washed away, Myers (w) qualifies the phrase "will again to live" by writing "Not reincarnation: Once only does the soul descend the way that leads to incarnation."

At some point Lodge said to the Myers (w) communicator, 'Why did you not give me exactly the same information that you gave Dorr originally from Ovid's *Metamorphoses?* The response was, 'If I had done that people would have said that it was just telepathy.'

(Author's note... you can't really win can you?)

Professor C. J. Ducasse, in his essay, "What would Constitute Conclusive Evidence of Survival?" was very impressed by the Piper evidence alone and was not even in possession of the still more impressive experiment subsequently conducted by Lodge with Mrs Willett.

Lodge commented,

Is it the least plausible that Mrs Piper – a woman of limited education – not only herself had or had got by ESP the knowledge of the recondite details of Ovid's writings required for the allusions made by the purported Myers – some of which knowledge Dorr did not himself have; but in addition herself had and exercised the capacity which Myers had so to combine these allusions as to make them say together tacitly about Lethe something which Myers knew, but which was other than any of the other things which, singly, those allusions referred to; and which it took Piddington [an intelligent and long-term student of the scripts] much study and thought to identify?

Mrs Verrall, who was involved with all of this, and who was a lecturer in classics at Newnham College, stated that she herself did not have the appropriate knowledge to easily evaluate the script writings of Mrs Piper. It therefore seems most unlikely to me then that Mrs Piper would understand them to any extent at all.

If anyone actually takes the trouble to go to the relevant PSPR volumes and read therein the developments of the Lethe case, additional important matters are brought to their attention. Firstly it is apparent that Sir Oliver Lodge and Mrs Verrall were continually and honestly striving at every stage to find normal explanations for the scripts and statements produced by Mrs Willett, even to the extent of testing quite ridiculous and highly improbable 'normal' scenarios, and not finding any to fit. Secondly it is apparent that the communicator, whoever or whatever he is, is often indulging in a two-way 'dialogue' with Sir Oliver Lodge and displaying the intelligence, the classical knowledge and the characteristic idiosyncrasies of the Myers that Lodge and Verrall had known when he was alive. And thirdly and sadly, the Lodge and Verrall very long papers on the Lethe Case are good examples of the extremely valuable researches to be found in contemporary publications of the SPR; researches that are now unknown to the vast majority of modern psychical researchers and parapsychologists.

Montague Keen, David Fontana and Archie Roy rightly, I believe, looked upon the Lethe Case as a case of such evidential power of the paranormal in operation. The fact is that it makes it necessary to take very seriously indeed the possibility that human personality in some way survives bodily death, and it poses a severe challenge to the fundamental sceptic who denies that any paranormal phenomenon has ever been proven to occur. These researchers, among others, have offered many challenges to sceptics to provide a convincing normal explanation for this case. To the best of my knowledge, no normal explanation has been proffered!

In 1917 Mrs Eleanor Sidgwick admitted that the Cross-Correspondences, which were still continuing and would do so for another 13 years, had convinced her that survival of death took place. In her cool, succinct and intelligent way she wrote of the relationship between a pair of automatists:

> We have to seek the designer. It cannot be the supraliminal (i.e. conscious) intelligence of either automatist, since ex hypothesi, neither of them is aware of the design until it is completed. Nor, for a similar reason, can it be attributed to some other living person, since, so far as can be ascertained, no other living person had any knowledge of what was going on. It is extremely difficult to suppose that the design is an elaborate plot of the subliminal (i.e. subconscious) intelligence of either or both automatists acting independently and without any knowledge on the part of the supraliminal consciousness; and the only remaining hypothesis seems to be that the designer is an external influence, not in the body." She concluded: "I must admit that the general effect of the evidence on my own mind is that there is cooperation with us by friends and former fellow-workers no longer in the body.

So who was the designer (or designers) of the scripts? Who made the selection of the material transmitted in the communications? The key word is 'Selection'. Who would have been able to make the selection?

Mrs Sidgwick's words are reminiscent of a Myers (w) statement made in 1910. On June 5th, Myers (w) emphasises the importance of the material that was selected for inclusion in Mrs Willett's script. He, almost teasingly, addressed to the investigator J. G. Piddington words that may fitly conclude this chapter:

> 'Write the word Selection.
> Who selects, my friend Piddington?
> I address this question to Piddington.
> Who selects?'

As far as Myers is concerned this certainly appears to be one of the 'Things that he could do when he was dead.'

Direct Voice Phenomena

When a séance is held with the intention of communicating with the departed, along with information coming from the medium, materialisation and other phenomena, direct voice can also occur. This means that a voice is heard which does not come directly from the medium or a materialised figure within that circle. It does not appear to be formed by the medium's vocal chords or larynx, giving the effect that the voice is coming from 'mid-air' or even from another part of that room.

One of the best known direct voice mediums was a man called Leslie Flint. He was not an affluent man; he did not have a particularly good childhood. His mother did not particularly want him and therefore left him to be raised by his Grandmother. He soon learned that he had to be self-sufficient in this life.

Leslie knew nothing about mediumship whatsoever but even as a child he displayed mediumistic abilities.

He came in from school one day and heard voices coming from the kitchen, one being his Grandmother's and the other the voice of woman unknown to him. He stuck his head around the door of the kitchen and saw that his grandmother was sitting in her chair and a woman with a large mole on her chin was standing beside her. As he watched them the other woman vanished, poof – disappeared.

He later asked his grandmother who she had been talking to and she said that she had been alone all afternoon. He described the woman that he had seen and got clouted on the ear. He mentioned the mole that the woman had on her chin and got clouted again because the response was, "That's Mrs Pugh and she has been dead and buried for a month or more." After that he learned to keep quiet.

As a young man he saw, what turned out to be, his recently deceased Uncle Alf in the kitchen. A friend said afterwards, "It was in your mind boy."

Leslie was puzzled as he rationalised to himself, "I never saw Uncle Alf in my whole life so how could I imagine him? I didn't even know that it was he until, at a later date, Aunt Nell showed me the snapshot of him that she found in his kitbag.

As a result of his self-sufficiency he managed to acquire many "interesting" jobs in his life.

As a young man, Leslie obtained one job in a graveyard and another as a film projectionist – a job that he absolutely loved as he was a huge film fan. This was around the time of transition from silent movies to "talkies."

One morning, while attending to tidying up the grounds in the graveyard, he noticed a gravestone that had not been cared for; in fact it was quite dilapidated. Leslie felt sorry for the person whose body was in that lair and decided to tidy it up. After he cut the grass and weeds away he brushed the stone and was somewhat surprised to find that the name on it was that of his old teacher, Edwin Lewis. He continued tidying up nearby when he saw a woman, carrying a large bunch of flowers, going to another gravestone. She removed an older bunch from the vase in front of that stone and inserted the new. She left the old flowers lying on the grass. As the old flowers still looked fresh enough to him he picked them up, found an old jam jar, filled it with water, popped the flowers into it and placed it beneath the headstone at Edwin Lewis's grave.

Around this time he was hopping from church to church looking for some kind of spiritual answer and a meaning to life but was despairing of any solution when a "speaker" in a conventional church warned the congregation "off" visiting spiritualists.

That was it – the warning stimulated Leslie's curiosity and off he went to "Visit these spiritualists with their low vibrations", whatever that meant!

On his first visit to a spiritualist church he was somewhat alarmed to find that the chairperson looked like (the murderer) Crippen and Leslie was becoming very unsure of the whole affair.

This uncertainty turned to alarm when the female medium later came to him during the service and thanked him for the flowers that he had put on Edwin Lewis's grave that morning!

This was the beginning for him; a spark was there and after a time he found himself in a spiritualist home circle.

On his first visit to this circle he thought that he had fallen asleep and was about to apologise, but it became obvious that he had spoken to individuals, while in a deep trance state, and all of the information that he had given was accurate.

This is reminiscent of the Hannen Swaffer circle, where a young man, Maurice Barbanell, who was an atheist, attended that home circle to mock the proceedings.

He laughed outright when the medium told him that he would be doing 'this' one day.

Although Barbanell was sceptical he returned the following week. He also thought that he had fallen asleep, but was in fact in a trance state. This eventually resulted in marvellous dialogues between the sitters and a spiritual teacher called Silver Birch, who spoke through Barbanell. The subsequent events resulted in the production of several wonderful books.

As an addendum, the books produced around the teaching of Silver Birch are very matter of fact and filled with common sense; I find difficulty in disagreeing with the philosophy therein.

Like Leslie Flint, Barbanell had been speaking in trance.

In Flint's case his mediumship developed into direct voice.

One set of critics put forward the theory that the voices heard by sitters in his direct voice circle were not real but, through a combination of hypnotic power on the medium's part and a subconscious longing on the part of the sitters, auditory hallucinations were produced.

As far as Flint was concerned, this glib theory was knocked on the head in 1948 when a gramophone record was made of a Flint circle séance and every voice came out very clearly on the record!

Around this time researchers from the SPR tested Flint.

The general protocol was as follows:

> His lips were sealed with *Elastoplast (Band-Aid)*.
> A throat microphone was attached to him and wired to amplifiers.
> The researchers observed the proceedings by means of an infrared telescope.
> His hands were held by a sitter on each side.

Among the witnesses were the Rev. Drayton Thomas and Brigadier R. C. Firebrace.

The Rev. Drayton Thomas gave the following account of the first of his experiments with Flint, which was held in the premises of the Society for Psychical Research, London.

'I placed over his tightly closed lips a strip of Elastoplast. It was five and a half inches long and two and a half inches wide and had very strong adhesive. This I firmly pressed over and into the crevices of the closed lips. A scarf was then tied tightly over this and the medium's hands tied firmly to the arms of the chair; another cord was so tied that he would be unable to bend down his head.'

Subsequently Drayton Thomas also enlisted the help of another psychical researcher who was an electronics expert in further experimentation. Sadly the identity of this person cannot easily be found. Some tests were carried out at this person's flat and others, yet again, at the premises of the SPR. When the electronics expert was present the séance protocol was as follows.

Flint's lips were sealed with Elastoplast. On some occasions water would also be put in his mouth.

A throat microphone was attached to him and wired to amplifiers so that the slightest sound made through Flint's larynx would be greatly magnified.

The researchers were able to watch every movement in the séance by means of an infrared telescope.

Flint's hands were held by sitters on each side of him. Nevertheless independent direct voices were heard, providing relevant information to individual sitters.

Under these test conditions and on more than one occasion a researcher, viewing through the infrared telescope, reported that they could see what looked like an 'ectoplasmic' larynx forming on the left side of Flint some two feet away from him. This appeared to be the vicinity of the source of the discarnate voices.

Drayton Thomas's evaluation of Flint's mediumistic abilities was that, 'Leslie Flint had absolutely no part in producing the voices.'[14]

I know that the people who sat in Flint's circles were completely convinced that they were speaking to their, son, daughter, parent, or other loved one. I have interviewed one or two of them.

Although some people speculate about the method of production of these voices, I do not.

There is no actual evidence to support any particular uniform theory – (unless you know differently – and I would be more than happy to examine that evidence.)

Nonetheless, in the absence of precise theory and methodology, the amount of well researched evidence collected still points to the reality of this phenomenon.

This was Leslie Flint's experience.

Arthur Findlay, the well respected and wealthy Scottish businessman, was convinced of the reality of survival only after hearing direct voice in the John Sloan circle, in Glasgow.

Quote by Findlay: "After 39 séances with John Sloan, for which he refused any payment, I was satisfied, after applying every test I could think of, that the voices were not those of the medium or any other earth person present."

---

[14] Ref www.tanika.com/04-mediums/flint.htm

Within this circle Arthur Findlay also received accurate information, by means of direct voice, from, among others, his father; information that no one else could have known.

Arthur Findlay was nobody's fool.

As with all other topics, I stress again that I am considering specific phenomena which have some substance – not fraudulent or delusional material. I have no doubt there have been many examples of fraudulent or deluded people.

Chapter 14

PARANORMAL HEALING

Paranormal healing can and does work. You only have to study the work of Harry Edwards, Arigo, George Chapman, and many others to see pragmatic results.

Around 2006 I was fortunate to come across two modern healers who appeared to be achieving good results. This resulted in a five year study of these healers, who work independently of each other, and I now offer you some testimonies and reports from this study. The two healers concerned are Gary Mannion and Nina Knowland.

Patient 1
Woman in her 50's

"For some time I had problems with severe pain in my side after eating. The pain was so bad at times that I had to be admitted to hospital for intravenous pain killers. I am an RGN and, as I expected, an ultrasound confirmed that I had gallstones. It was suggested that surgery to remove my gall bladder was the only really effective way of ensuring that the pain would not return. I was advised that a low fat diet might help to reduce the likelihood of the pain returning and I was also advised that I would need to lose weight before surgery was safe. As the pain didn't seem to be relieved with diet restrictions, I decided to see

Nina after hearing that she had had success with other similar problems. Nina placed her hands on my side over my "gall bladder" and the area became hot and I felt a pulling and a "popping" sensation. She gave me healing for about 10-15 minutes. Immediately after seeing Nina I did not have any problems with pain and at a follow up ultrasound the radiographer couldn't see any gall stones present."

Patient 2
Man aged 36

Shane fell off a forklift truck and landed on his coccyx. He attended his doctor, Dr Trowel, who said that it was probably sciatica and he advised him to take strong painkillers. He was off work for two weeks with the severe pain and about 4 weeks later a large bruise appeared on and around his coccyx. His back was very painful. He went to see Nina and he declared that within about 26 seconds, "It was as though I was under an anaesthetic, although there was no smell of ether, I was dead to the world. After 20-30 minutes of healing I got instant relief and have had little bother since. It becomes a little bit sore from time to time, but nothing like the intense pain that was there before." Shane is convinced that Nina healed him.

Nina said that there was an abscess at the bottom of his back – but there is no actual evidence to confirm this.

Patient 3
Woman in her 70's

Nina had known Mary for some years but had not seen her for a long time. She literally bumped into a lady in the street and was shocked to discover that it was Mary, as Nina did not recognise her because she was so thin. Mary explained that she had been constantly sick for about 3 months, could not keep any food down, and had gone from 8 stone to 5 stone in the 3 month period. She was now a size 6. The doctors diagnosed hiatus hernia. She had recently been admitted to hospital for a week and was, quote, "Worse when she came out."

Nina took her to her place of work and gave her healing. Mary felt the sensation of heat from Nina's hands along with a tingling sensation and a feeling of internal movement within her body. She left Nina's and went home to cook dinner for her husband. She also cooked some for herself, ate the whole lot and kept it down. She has never been sick since and is now, some six months later, nearly up to 10 stone. She went back to the hospital for a check-up and had a scope again put down her gullet. The doctor could not find anything wrong and was most perplexed. His perplexity would not have been helped by the fact that Mary told him that a spirit doctor had operated on her and that she was instantly cured!!

I asked Mary if she thought that Nina had cured her condition and her reply was, "Nina saved my Life!"

Patient 4
Man in his 30's
Occupation: self-employed plasterer.

The patient's eye was "glassed" in a pub fight. A Guinness pint glass was smashed on a bar and thrust into his face. He was rushed to hospital and kept in for a week. His eye had virtually been cut in half. The first operation took 6 hours and the doctors had to cut through 18 layers to remove the glass that was in his eye. He was told that they had done the best that they could but they might have to remove his eye. The doctor also told him that it was the worst eye injury that he had ever seen. The retina had detached, and both pupil and iris were destroyed. One week later they explained that they would definitely have to remove the eye as a great pressure had built up in it, and removal would prevent any ensuing infection from travelling to the other eye. The patient was less than pleased.

They allowed him to go home. By that time he had actually selected his artificial eye for a proposed operation on the following Wednesday.

As it was extremely painful he visited Nina on the following Sunday for pain relief. At that point she did not have a lot of time to spend with him, but spent enough time with him to relieve the pain.

Next day, on the Monday, he made a visit to the hospital for a final check before the scheduled op on the Wednesday.

On Tuesday he went to Nina's for a longer healing.

I asked him to describe the healing.

"Apart from any further pain removal, it felt as if something was knitting away at the back of my eye. I could picture my Nan with her knitting needles and it felt like that." The healing lasted about 30 minutes.

Shaun had said to Nina, "I don't care if I am blind in that eye as long as I don't have to have it removed."

When he appeared at the hospital the next day the doctors examined his eye prior to removal and were somewhat surprised that the pressure in the eye had returned to normal and the retina had re-attached. The doctors decided that they no longer had to remove the eye.

He still has no sight in this eye, but it does move in conjunction with the other eye and it does not look at all peculiar. He emphasised again to me that he really did not want to lose his eye – that was of prime importance.

I asked him, "Do you believe that Nina saved your eye?" His reply was, "Without a doubt."

He also told me that if he had had to get an artificial eye that he would have killed himself, as he would only have felt half a man. Therefore in his opinion, Nina saved his life.

Patient 5
Shelly -Woman aged 33
Date of testimony June 2006

In Sept 2005 the patient, while at work, had great difficulty in standing up and eventually had to get help to go home. She was then taken to hospital by ambulance where she was bed bound for a week. They were not sure if it was a slipped disc or a trapped nerve. She was given a support belt and returned home on crutches and given the use of a wheelchair and a commode. Two weeks later her back had improved.

In May 2006 the condition returned – the pain was unbearable. In June 2006 she met Nina and asked her if she could help with the pain. She saw her that evening. To get to Nina, Shelly had to be helped into her car and have someone fit the seatbelt. When she arrived at Nina's she was bent over at an angle and dependent on crutches. Nina said that she would have to try to straighten her back so that she could get her onto the couch. "Placing her hands on my spine she asked me to gently try to straighten up my back, I was holding on to the back of her chair. Gradually I was able to stand up straight. The nerve was still trapped and it made me jump. When I was eventually straight she asked me to lie on the couch and she put her hands above where the nerve was trapped. Nina was able to release the nerve and it also felt as if a disc had been put back into place. When I got off the couch I had no pain.

Nina asked me to try to sit on the dining chair and then the armchair; again I had no pain. I was able to climb up into my 4x4 straight away. I was also able to reach round and put the seatbelt on. I have had no pain since that day and am now able to work. I would definitely recommend Nina for her healing."

Patient 6
Woman age 36

The patient attended Nina on the 26th November 2002, when she was 31. I video interviewed this patient in April 2008. The patient had attended for pain relief.

She always had agonising and heavy menstrual periods, since the age of 18. The pain was so bad that it would make her physically sick. On a couple of occasions she even fainted and it would often also give her diarrhoea. Her doctor prescribed the contraceptive pill, thinking that it might help, but it made no difference. The whole condition was affecting her work as she would frequently have to have several days off. This was not popular in a male environment. She had a healing from Nina at a time when she was about to start a period and while she was in great pain.

Quote from patient: "You came to visit and placed your hands over my lower stomach area and at a time when a period was about to start. I felt a very warm sensation as if something was being moved about inside. Within 10 minutes the pain had subsided enough to be "bearable" and within half an hour there was no more pain." When the healing was completed and the patient stood up, her light-headedness was gone. It has been six years since that healing and she has been to no other healer or doctor since. She has NEVER had another excruciating painful menstrual cycle.

Patient 7
Woman aged 29
20/10/09

'When I was 17, I was admitted to hospital for an emergency operation for which the initial diagnosis was appendicitis: my appendix was removed and there proved to be nothing wrong with it. It turned out to be a ruptured cyst on my left ovary which resulted in two pints of blood loss with internal bleeding. This second operation was a major one and left me with a large scar on my lower abdomen with internal scarring and trauma. Following this, and it has been over 12 years since that operation, I have had numerous problems with this area of my body including IBS, irregular periods, polycystic ovaries, haemorrhoids, ongoing and various digestive complaints, upset bowels when menstruating and a lot of discomfort therein.'

'During the session with Nina I felt a number of sensations: heat travelling in what felt like channels, up from where her hands were placed, and fairly central to my torso, head and neck. There were feelings of things moving around inside, not only where her hands were placed, but in other areas that felt they were connected. There was some 'bubbling' in my stomach when she was working on my lower back/base of spine. This is what I can remember now; sorry if I'm forgetting anything. Not even two weeks have passed and my haemorrhoids have gone and I had a normal cycle with my period, with no upset bowels or discomfort from the start of my last menstruation. The session has helped tremendously. I am very glad I went to Nina and I am recommending people I know to go and see her for their health conditions.'

I spoke to the Patient 3/5/10. (Approx. 7 months after the healing) The haemorrhoids have not returned and the other conditions do not feel so severe. She is hoping to go back for another top-up healing.

Patient 8
Woman late 20's
Written Testimony 19th November 2009

'...During a healing for another condition, I noticed that my feet had suddenly gone numb.

I told Nina and she asked if I had any problems with my feet. I told her that I had recently been in hospital and had both feet broken and reset because the position of the feet was causing back problems. Both feet had been facing outwards, affecting my posture, so they needed to be straightened. The procedure involved cutting through the inside of each foot and inserting plates and pins. I was born with this condition but as I have got older the symptoms have steadily worsened. When Nina finished working on my stomach area she went to my feet. I couldn't feel her hands at all, even though Nina said they felt hot.

Then it felt like pin pricks all along the scar on my right foot, I didn't feel anything on the left, as my foot was totally numb. By the end of the healing I started to feel Nina's hands on both feet. After I got up from the bed I found I could move my toes, which I was very surprised about. I couldn't believe it. I hadn't been able to do that since the June prior to when I had the hospital operation. The following day my feet felt back to normal, only now they were straight, my posture was improved and I had no pain in my back.'

Update 12/5/10

"After the operation, the hospital had said that it would be 12 months before I would see any improvement in my feet and in walking and that I would never get full movement of the big toe again.

It is now 7 months since the operation and 6 months after having the healing with Nina. Since then my feet have just remained the same as after having the healing. Before the operation my foot was ridged; it was like wearing flippers because I couldn't bend my feet. I now have complete movement in them and have been able to buy loads of shoes including high heels. I had been experiencing pain in my feet continually since the operation but until now, after the healing, there are still no pains in my feet.

Patient 9

Woman, 57 – mother of the previous patient. Patient was in a wheelchair.
Healing date 5th Nov 2009
Condition: pulmonary blood clots in the lungs
Medication: Warfarin, Claxain, atenol, diltazem, prednisone.
Patient felt numb and as if a heavy square block was on her chest.
Testimony (written by her daughter)
19th November 2009

Mum had been into hospital for two weeks due to diagnosed pulmonary clots in her lung; this meant that she was unable to get out of bed during this time.' She was discharged on the 30th Sept 2009. The daughter then took her mother to see Nina.

'I told Nina mum had clots in her lung. Nina was deciding whether or not she should do a healing due to the seriousness of the condition. She decided to do the healing. She first put her hands on mum's back, straight away her lips turned from purple to red. I told mum. Nina continued with the healing by putting her hands below mum's breasts until her breathing became stable.

I drove mum home and stopped the car. I was getting her wheelchair out of the back of the car when I heard footsteps on the chippings. I looked up and mum was walking into the house! I asked her what she was doing. She replied, "I'm all right; I'm going in." She took herself up the stairs on the chairlift to the bathroom all by herself, which she doesn't normally do.

.......The next day mum was able to walk about and I even took her shopping. Mum went to the hospital on 11th November. They said there didn't seem to be any symptoms of the blood clots although due to mum's illness they couldn't x-ray to see if the blood clots had gone.

She has not got any symptoms that she had before; she is now going shopping; she walks about with her trolley which she couldn't do before. She is now able to take herself to the bathroom and go out of the house more than she could do before.'

I spoke to the daughter early 2010.

She said that her mother was amazing and gone from strength to strength. She also said that the doctors said they had no explanation for the recovery. (Hearsay of course)

Follow up testimony 19/5/10

"When Nina first gave mum healing.....she had been told by the consultant at Musgrove that she had a very short life expectancy left. They advised her to make a will as she was not expected to live for more than a couple of days.

During the healing mum could feel a sensation of pressure and heat on her front and back. On her second visit to mum's house, a week later, she felt a sensation of pushing down at the top of her chest, along her collarbone. A few weeks later mum went back into hospital with breathing difficulties. They already were aware she had (had) respiratory failure and blood clots. They were initially going to send her home. The doctors were not going to treat her because her heart rate was so high because of the clots, so I refused to take her home. They started her on a heart pill just to slow her heart down and make her comfortable. She was admitted because of a suspected chest infection; they did blood tests and they picked up that she had a problem with her thyroid gland. The thyroid problem was then diagnosed and treatment proposed....

Early May mum had an outpatient's appointment. The consultants were amazed at her improvement. And also her blood gases had increased from bottom 80's to 90's, which they were impressed with. The consultant had said to her it appeared that the reason she became so ill was because of the underlying thyroid problem they hadn't detected, because they were focussing on her other health conditions. So now they have the thyroid under control the future doesn't look so bleak for her. After she had an appointment to see the thyroid specialist, they started treatment and I brought her home, and she improved a lot, then she had another appointment with the consultant who then said perhaps it wasn't clots at all. What they said to cover themselves was... 'the clots must have dispersed themselves or they weren't there in the first place, which then enabled them to treat the thyroid condition.' Following her appointment in May 2010 the consultant sent a copy of a letter sent to her Dr which said that he was amazed at the improvement of her condition and the improvement of her appearance... the outlook is now very good for her. Over the weekend mum has been walking around the garden without her trolley; she has slept all night Friday, Saturday and Sunday, which is unusual. Mum now doesn't need to stay in bed all day. Her skin colour is normal. She didn't go out before seeing Nina but now she goes out every day on her scooter. She also does not need a wheelchair unless we are walking a very long distance."

Since then they have stopped Warfarin, Atonal, Diltazim, Prednisone. Now she is taking Thyroxin, Carbimazole, Furosemide."

A research programme was set up in Glasgow by T J Robertson (me) on the 2nd and 3rd August 2008.

I, through advertising, provided all of the subjects for healing.

Many of these had very defined conditions with medical records available. All of the participants were video interviewed before and after the healing and post healing contact maintained, by TJR.

Healer: Gary Mannion
Interviewer: T J Robertson
Witness: Prof Archie Roy
Cameraman: Ian McEwan

About the healer: Through previous work with Gary, I have noted that he achieves great improvement in patients, which he attributes to psychic surgery. He states that his controls (surgeons) at this time are a man called Abraham and a woman, namely Dr Nicole Alexandra.

All of the patients' details are on file, but this report will be anonymous. The next two reports are from that controlled session on 2nd and 3rd August.

Patient 10

Woman aged 54 with a psychology degree and previous experience in nursing.

Condition requiring healing: extreme back pain – persisted for 10 years – patient awaiting result of a recent MRI scan from the Southern General Hospital, Glasgow. She does know that she has had a compound fracture in her back from an earlier time.

The healer told patient that her disc had "slipped out", before applying healing.

Post healing the subject said that it was quite extraordinary, as she did not know what to expect. First of all it felt like needles at the base of her back – "right on the spot where I feel my pain emanates from – and without me telling him. Now when you've had children you can put up with a lot of pain and I can tell you it wasn't extremely painful but there was definitely something going on. I felt as if someone was stitching and before that there was other pushing and pulling and I could feel like manipulation. He then went up to the initial fracture that I had, without direction, and I could feel the same again – but not as much manipulating but I could definitely feel the needles and it's not just that somebody's hands were on me. Gary's hands were above me. For me to have felt what I felt, he would have needed a whole medical kit with needles and knives and everything there for me to feel what I felt. He also told me that I have a wheat and dairy intolerance, and that was right. He said my weight was partly due to hormones and I know that's right, but my doctor refuses to believe it. I'm actually sore just now where he's been working but he did say that would happen for a few days."

Two days after the healing the patient reported: "I have been feeling a bit tender all weekend and still a bit sore, but not the same kind of sore that I had previously and I have to report that I am walking better, with no limp and less stiffness when standing up. I had despaired of ever getting back to my old self."

Later that day she received the result of her MRI scan, which confirmed that her disc (pre-healing) had "slipped out."

Under his hands the healer felt the sensations of vibrations, heat, tearing, and manipulation, as if the patient was being injected.

The healer felt that of his two controls it was Dr Nicole Alexandra who worked with this patient.

Approximately one week later the patient had further improved and can now lift her arms above her head – a task that she has been unable to perform for years.

On 26th August (24 days after healing) the patient wrote: "I went to see the surgeon yesterday and saw the pictures of the scan and where my spine had slipped out and was crushing my nerve. The surgeon had expected to operate and was quite surprised when I told him I was fine and back to my old self."

For many years later, this patient maintained the betterment that she achieved from this healing.

Patient 11
Man, aged 42
Musician

The patient was hoping for some improvement in eyesight, as he has had genetic glaucoma for the past 5 years and the condition is destined to deteriorate as he gets older. The condition increases eye pressure and this is one of the problems. The patient was given some drugs by his doctor, but it seemed to make his sight worse. (In his view.) He has lost more vision in one eye since diagnosis.

During the healing the patient felt very peaceful, very relaxed and a warm sensation, almost inside the eye, rather than outside. He could feel vibrations which he attributed to the healer's hands – no pain or discomfort – just a positive experience.

The healer felt more pressure on the right hand optic nerve, but not too much difference.

Healer felt as though he was cutting behind the eye, draining something away and had a sense, or feeling, of air escaping.

The patient was told that he should see some improvement in two weeks or so. He was also told that the control (healer) was Abraham.

On the 19th August, seventeen days after the healing, the patient reported:

"I feel my eyes became slightly sharper in vision 3 or 4 days leading up to my recent eye examination. To be fair to Gary he did tell me improvement could take a couple of weeks. Yesterday I had my eye check-up at Gartnavel Hospital (18th Aug). I always ask my eye pressure readings, normally around 16-18 in each eye. This time the eye pressure was lower – 14 in both eyes. The eye specialist also told me I had done slightly better in visual field tests in both eyes than the previous check-up 6 months ago. She showed me a few areas on the chart that I missed last time which I detected to some degree this time. I said to her, "Areas of lost vision due to glaucoma are not supposed to return, are they?" Her answer was along the lines ...... 'Well, people do better in tests sometimes than at other times.' So although not a big enough improvement to impress doctors, who have to assume it was just me doing worse in a previous test and just a day with lower eye pressure, I feel this is a good result and I am now feeling more optimistic that further improvements can occur." I spoke to the patient in December 2014 and his eyes had maintained the improvement enjoyed by the healing.

Patient 12
Man, Aged 30
Essex

He was involved in a car crash in Aug 1997 where he banged his head on the inside of the roof. There was even a visible bump on the roof on the outside of the car. He did not go for treatment. In Sept 1999 he became tired for no reason and was also getting sharp pains in his neck, from time to time. Sometimes he would dose on painkillers and be confined to bed. He was also not sleeping properly at this time. The Doctor prescribed anti-depressants and said that it would relax the brain and he could sleep easier. This made things worse. After several visits to the GP and trials of other medication she referred him to a neurologist. Different medications were tried, but nothing worked. Diagnosis – possible chronic fatigue syndrome.

This was now 2001.

In 2003 he tried some alternative therapies, which helped for a short time.

In 2004 he tried acupuncture, which did help for a day or two.

In 2005 he changed GP and was referred to a clinic. This didn't really help the condition and he also kept getting tonsillitis and flu symptoms.

In early 2008, (11 years after the crash) he attended Gary Mannion.

The patient experienced ice cold feelings and tingling whilst Gary's hands were on his back. He also felt very relaxed.

The healer told him that he would be very sore for the next few days and that he would be advised to come back for one more treatment.

"As soon as I got up from the couch treatment, my back felt very bruised and sore, but this pain went completely within a few days and I started to feel different. I made another appointment to see him a month or so later and after the second treatment my back and neck felt fine. I didn't have any pain as experienced the first time.

Since that visit to Gary my tiredness has virtually disappeared. I feel more alert and I no longer have any pain in my back and neck. In addition to this, I have noticed that the heels on my shoes have started to wear more evenly now than they were before I saw him. I also intend to see Gary again soon as my hay-fever is becoming a problem."

Patient 13
Woman aged 41
Cumbria

"During 2006 and into 2007 I was suffering from pain in my lower right side. Following numerous tests at the doctors, the cause remained unknown. At times I was crippled by the pain and lay flat on the floor for relief. On 12th August 2007 my mother visited Gary Mannion and she handed him a 'post-it' note with my name written on it, asking for his advice. He said that it was my kidney tubes. Following this, I re-visited the doctors on the 10th September 2007 and an appointment was made for me to have an ultrasound scan at the local hospital. The ultrasound scan showed that the right kidney tube was dilated and suggested further tests were needed to find out what was happening to my kidney. The pain and lethargy continued.

On the 4th October 2007 I visited Gary and received a 20 minute 'treatment' where he confirmed his previous diagnosis and added that the kidney was functioning by only 10%. He told me that the healing would continue over the coming days. During the month that followed the pain lessened to such an extent that the pain disappeared completely and my energy levels soared.

The referral came through from the hospital for another CT scan on the 21st November 07, which I attended. The CT scan showed fully functioning kidneys and tubes and neither the radiographer nor the doctor were able to diagnose anything further from the scan. (Doctors letters are held by TR.)

Patient 14
Woman aged 25
East Sussex,

"I have been disabled since the age of 6/7 and diagnosed with chronic fatigue syndrome. At the age of 11, I was diagnosed with Fibromyalgia and when I was 18 (after 8 years of severe chronic pain), I was diagnosed with endometriosis.

I have had numerous treatments and operations to treat these conditions but nothing has ever worked long term. In 2006 I was rushed to hospital and we discovered that I also had renal stones. After 2 operations within 7 weeks to try to manually break up the stones in my kidney, I was discharged, only to find within 7 months I was back in hospital for more surgery to remove stones from my other kidney. By December 07, I was going back to the hospital again weekly for tests and scans. By February 08 I had all of the three major health conditions that I was dealing with on a daily basis, and then there was also the pain from my kidneys as if I had stones for the third time in 2 years. At this point I was taking morphine on a daily basis. I saw Gary in March and have seen him 4 times in 5 months. I have to say that I have not experienced this kind of healing before and, although a believer in alternative remedies, I was slightly sceptical as I like to see proof. Well it didn't take long for the proof to show. I felt better overall from my first treatment and have now come off painkillers – like the morphine I have been on for a very long while. I am able to do more with my life now – day by day I feel I am growing stronger and able to do more and more. My life has completely turned around in just less than 6 months and, even though I'm not in good health, I am in the best position health wise I have been in since I was 5/6 years old.

When people ask me what I am doing seeing Gary I simply answer with, it is something that is unexplainable and must be tried. I am not usually one to sing praises but I really feel that he has helped me and

I cannot thank him enough. I feel that I have a life now. I give my full consent for you to allow this testimonial to be used as evidence."

Patient 15
Young man – 30's
Master Instructor Choi Kwang Do Martial Arts, B.A. Eng Hons

"In March 2005 I injured my lower back whilst stretching (in yoga the posture is known as *Supta Virasana*); I essentially did not warm up correctly prior to performing this specific stretch. At the time I knew I had injured myself and my thoughts were confirmed as I felt pain in my lower back the next day. However, since I had never suffered with any type of back pain before, I just brushed it off, putting it down as a slight ache which would get better in a day or two. However, as the days weeks and months went by, my back pain progressively began to worsen and, as the years began to pass, I was now termed as a chronic back pain sufferer.

In the early months of 2007 I decided that this pain needed to be arrested and so I sought the help of many qualified alternative therapists and therapies, Acupuncture, Bowen, Chiropractic and Physiotherapy. Unfortunately at the time none of these treatments seemed to work. You may be wondering, 'Why did I wait so long before seeking help?' and the answer is that I believe (and still do) that the body can heal itself and that with correct back strengthening exercises (after muscles have been released), good diet and positive thought, I would be able to heal myself. One thing that I was absolutely certain of was that I was NOT going to have conventional back surgery.

It was now the end of November 2007 and the pain in my back was excruciating. In the past I had always thought that back sufferers were somewhat melodramatic often 'making a mountain out of a molehill' as the saying goes. However I now have total empathy; I would dread the experience of having to do simple mundane daily functions such as sneezing, coughing, walking, sitting and even getting out of bed. As I was now at the threshold of my pain tolerance, my mind was such that I would do anything to get just a little bit of relief; I was seriously thinking of having a private back operation. In December 2007 a friend of mine introduced me to Gary Mannion; he said that he was a Psychic Surgeon and that he would be able to 'fix me.' Being completely honest, I thought, 'What is this young boy going to do for me, plus the fact that I am not a believer in psychic phenomena.'

Well how wrong could I have been; after a 15 minute session with Gary I was about 80% free from pain; I could not believe it. Abraham, through Gary, said that my lower vertebra L5 had collapsed and the one above it L4 had a considerable amount of wear. This was exactly what my MRI scan had shown. He also said that because of the injury a nerve had become trapped and badly damaged – its colour was grey instead of being a healthy white colour. Gary/Abraham 'pushed this disc back into place and released the trapped nerve. Abraham prescribed some stretching exercises for me to rebuild the damaged nerve and with that the surgery was completed. I would like to thank Gary for healing this injured body of mine and I wholeheartedly recommend Gary. Please keep up the good work."

I don't want to editorialise any of these accounts, but please do not dismiss them as fantasy, as at least they should give you food for thought. If they are all instant remissions, isn't it strange how all of the patients achieved this immediately after a healing?

You know the old saying: Don't knock it 'til you've tried it.

Note: A full report of the 64 page healing study can be found under 'Ostensible Paranormal Healing' on my website www.triciarobertson. weebly.com

Chapter 15

A POTPOURRI OF PARANORMALITY

There are so many facets to paranormal activity that no one person can know everything about, or indeed examine, every topic in depth. The following short examples illustrate the type of things that happen to ordinary people in everyday life.

Roger

In 2013, Roger Smith (pseudonym) related the following to me in the 'off air' time during a radio programme in which I was the guest.

His sister has a little girl who was between two and three at the time of this event. His sister often heard her daughter speaking out loud, as if in conversation in her room, but didn't think too much of it until one day she asked her who she was talking to. She said, 'The nice man with the brown dog who sometimes comes to see me.'

Roger's father had died before the little girl was born and there were no photographs of him in that family's home. This surprise statement from the girl somewhat startled the mother who wasn't quite sure of what to do or say. It sounded very like her father. She subsequently showed her daughter a wide selection of old family photos. From these she immediately pointed out the man that she had been speaking to in her room, plus the dog, which was a Doberman mix. This dog had been devoted to the father while they were both alive.

If this was just one account of such a thing then we may happily dismiss it as a child's fantasy, but it is most certainly not.

Diane

A friend of mine recently related the following account. It concerns her great grandson who would be three in the following January.

'His Mum phoned my daughter Margaret, (pseudonym), to say that the child seemed to be talking to someone in the hall and what should she do. I suggested that she should ask him whom he was talking to. At this point I have to tell you that my grandchildren called my Mum GiGi, but this great grandchild has never heard this name, as mum died a long time ago. When his mum asked who he was talking to, he said it was a lady who said her name was GiGi and that she was his gran.

The next time the family visited Margaret, she brought out some old photos and asked him if the lady that he was speaking to was in any of them, and with no hesitation, he picked out my mum straight away.

Thought this might interest you. He may lose this gift as he grows up, but we will see.'

Granddaughter

Because of my interest in the paranormal I have never forced my opinions or many experiences onto my children. They will have to find their own life paradigms.

When my granddaughter was about three her mother was getting her ready for bed, downstairs in the house. The child seemed distracted and kept looking up at the lounge curtains and smiling. My daughter said:

'Why are you smiling at the curtains?'

Reply: 'I'm smiling at the lady.'

Daughter: (after giving it some thought) 'Have you seen this lady before?'

Reply: 'Yes, she comes to my room (upstairs) and talks to me.'

Daughter: (after further thought) 'Do you know who this lady is?'

Reply: (with slight disdain) 'Yes...... she told me Granny is her daughter.'

As you may all guess, I am Granny, not Gran, Nan, or any other name. My mother died in 2002, granddaughter born in 2005. There are no photos of my mother in view in their house, or indeed mine.

I think that this gave my daughter food for thought. The child was not bothered one way or another.

Robert (pseudonym)

This relates to a friend of a friend, whose wife died fairly young, about 20 years ago. This man never believed in or thought of life after death or any of the implications of such an idea. He was not coping very well after her passing and feeling very, very, sorry for himself.

About six months after her death he was sitting in bed, reading in a good light, when his wife appeared at the side of his bed; solid, in colour and fully dressed. She sat on the side of his bed and he felt the bed depress. Forthcoming was not a compassionate utterance or sentimental words that one might have reasonably expected, but she launched into the following.

Wife: 'Here you, stop feeling sorry for yourself.' This was accompanied by patting him several times on his upper arm, fairly forcefully. 'Life is like a book and our chapter is over; close that book and start a new one.' She stayed for about 15 minutes during which they had further conversation.

If he had been looking for a contact with his wife this would certainly not have been his chosen dialogue. He knows that he was absolutely awake.

Unfortunately he did not really take her advice and I hope that he does not read this book!

Visitor

A couple of years ago I was giving a talk about apparitions to a group of about 25 people, most of whom I knew. During the talk I asked the audience if anyone had seen an apparition and whether or not it was entire, partial, semi-solid, see-through, solid, black and white or in colour.

One or two people related their experiences but the one that stood out for me was that of a lady whom I had never seen before or, for that matter, since. She looked quite young to me and I did not expect the content of her account.

Approximately two years earlier her husband had died. About a year after that she was in bed reading, once again in a good light and wide awake, when her husband appeared as a solid apparition in the bedroom and looked directly at her.

I asked, 'What did you do?'

Woman: (W) 'I ran screaming out of the bedroom into the lounge.'

Me: 'Why did you do that?'

W: 'Well I shouted at him, you shouldn't be here; you're dead!'

Me: 'What did you do then?'

W: 'For the next year I slept on the sofa in the lounge with the light on.'

Me: 'Why?'

W: 'I was frightened that he would come back.'

Not sensing that this was a marriage made in heaven, I did not pursue the matter any further.

Responsibility

A few years ago I was called to a house where a young woman was very upset and I didn't really know why I was there, only that she was an emotional mess.

The following account gradually revealed itself.

She was married and had a very nice husband. About 10 years earlier this girl had her first child in a local hospital. The child had minor problems, according to the hospital, and they told the woman to go home. During that night the child took a turn for the worse and died. The woman was obviously distressed and an added stress would be that she was not there when the baby passed. She was asked at the time if she would give the baby's body to science and in her confused state she agreed.

You are wondering what this has to do with anything.

Not very long before I attended this house she was shocked to receive a call from the hospital to say that they had now finished with the baby's body and she was now free to arrange a funeral.

They also told her that the baby's brain was the only part that had been used for science.

The funeral was arranged and some time passed. During this time, and even before this, she had attended a few spiritualist meetings but had never received any 'word' about the baby who had passed over.

Just before she called me she had gone for a private sitting with a (so called) local medium in the medium's house. She explained the situation and the medium said, 'Oh the reason that you haven't heard from your baby is that he has no brain.' The girl was devastated and inconsolable to think that she had deprived her child of an existence after death.

While the girl was telling me all of this she was shaking and in a terrible state. My reaction was one of pure anger at this irresponsible medium. I explained to her that that there was a wealth of documented cases of people who had died in plane crashes, car crashes, wars, etc. where there was really nothing left of the physical body, but communication had still been shown to take place.

I was so angry that, after reassuring the girl that this medium's assessment of the situation was absolute nonsense, I phoned Gordon Smith, the medium, who was still hairdressing at the time. My reason for this was that I knew that the girl probably needed more than one sensible person to pass an opinion.

Gordon agreed that this was nonsense but was unfortunately with a client when I phoned him and he couldn't really speak. When my anger settled down a bit I asked the girl if she now had children. She said yes, a boy and a girl. I asked her if either child had ever said anything strange along paranormal lines. After some thought she said that when her son was smaller he used to say that he had been here before.

I put forward the idea that the reason that she had not heard anything about the first baby was that, just maybe, he was back with her now. A switch had been flipped. She stopped shaking and sobbing and just stared at me. I had obviously given her food for thought. I knew that my word alone would not be enough for anyone who had been so traumatised.

I then arranged for her to have a sitting with Mr Charles Morton, a spiritualist minister. I did not tell Charles anything about her circumstances.

As she was still a bit fragile, I met her on the day of the sitting and took her to Charles's door. I came back for her about an hour later to find a smiling face. I have no idea what Charles told her, but our combined efforts seemed to do the trick.

A short time later she sent both of us a lovely card to thank us for our help.

She would not tell me the name of that medium who so upset her – maybe just as well!!

With mediumship comes great responsibility.

Hotel

As indicated previously, there can be humorous aspects to psychical investigations.

One such account to illustrate this is the following of an allegedly haunted hotel, as told to me by the hotel owner himself.

A new owner had taken over the operation of a hotel that had a reputation for strange occurrences in the form of paranormal phenomena. The new owner did not believe a word of these tales and dismissed it all as hearsay and nonsense. Upon taking over the hotel he began refurbishment of the said property and included in the staff that he employed to assist with this refurbishment was a young man who was not so sure that all the stories were false. Through circumstances, that particular young man was required to "live in" the hotel while refurbishment work was being undertaken. Unfortunately, you may say for him, he was given accommodation in one of the rooms that held a "spooky" reputation. This room was located at the very top of the building. During the first two nights of his stay there he did not get much sleep; as one eye was kept open all night while he noted every creak and other noise that he could hear in the building.

The third morning during this refurbishment period, the owner arose very early and, being a pleasant morning, he stepped outside to view his property. When he did this he noticed that a television aerial had fallen down flat onto the roof and needed to be returned to the vertical position. He decided to climb up this fairly high structure himself to rectify the situation. This he did and duly fixed the aerial.

Unfortunately, when he looked down he did not fancy the prospect of going back the same way as he had come up as it looked (and was) very steep and dangerous. He then remembered that there was an unused store-room that he could access from the roof as long as the window was unlatched, which he was sure that it was. Joy of joys, he reached the window, opened it, jumped into that room and landed with a bit of a thud on its wooden floor. It was then that he realised that this room was adjacent to the bedroom in which the nervous young man lay. It also dawned on him that behind the door from which he would have to exit this room was a wardrobe on the young man's side that would be blocking his way out. There was nothing else for it, he opened the adjoining door on his side to view the back of a wardrobe which was in fact directly facing the foot of the young man's bed.

I ask you now to imagine the scenario from a different standpoint, that of the young man. He is lying in bed, nervous and with one eye practically open all of the time, and he then hears a loud thud; now you can bet that his two eyes are open wide. The owner on the other side of the door has now had to push the wardrobe forward at one side to gain access to the room. In order to do this he had put one hand around the outside of one edge of the wardrobe, thus making his hand visible to the young man lying in his bed. The lad watched the wardrobe coming forward towards him. This was too much. The young man leapt from his bed and ran screaming from the room, through the corridors, down the stairs of the premises and out into the main street. To make matters worse, the young man had been sleeping without a stitch of clothes on and did not take time to rectify the situation before exiting the hotel!

I'm not sure if he ever came back.

Psychic Art

Psychic art can take different forms. It can be classified as a type of mediumship.

Many people purport to draw images of people who have passed on and often provide a mediumistic message, relating to this person, to a sitter while they draw.

Other people claim to be inspired to draw, or paint, under the influence of a deceased personality.

One of the strangest and well attested to, productions of psychic art come from two American ladies, the Bang sisters.

The Bang Sisters

The Bang sisters were actually physical mediums, not psychic artists in the generally accepted sense. (As I have said many times already, nothing in this genre is straightforward)

The first recorded demonstration of their precipitated art was in 1894 and was in the form of ink on paper. A sitter would bring along a sealed envelope which contained a blank sheet of paper. These were the days when little bottles of ink were used when writing a letter. The sitter would place the sealed envelope in front of the sisters, who never touched it, and after a time a scratching sound would be heard – as if coming from the inside of the envelope. During this time the sitter, and anyone else present, could observe the ink level slowly drop in the bottle, which was in full view, as the scratching sound continued. When the envelope was opened the paper inside contained a hand written letter from a deceased person. This was in the handwriting of that person and signed with an appropriate signature at the end.

Vice-Admiral William Usborne Moore, who was Queen Victoria's cartographer, diligently investigated the Bang sisters. As a cartographer he was practised in keeping immaculate records and he was, of course, a keen observer. After seeing the work of the sisters he contacted Sir William Crookes, who was a chemist, and asked him to prepare an ink which incorporated ingredients not normally associated with this type of ink. He subsequently presented himself to the Bang sisters, along with a sealed envelope and his own bottle of Crookes' 'special' ink. He had asked their permission to use this ink in the experiment and they readily agreed that this should not pose a problem. The usual routine took place resulting in a hand written letter being taken out of the sealed envelope after the session. Usborne Moore then sent that letter to Sir William Crookes for analysis. Crookes confirmed that the ink on the letter was indeed the ink that he had prepared.

After an unspecified time, the sisters developed work with oil paints.

The sitters would sit in front of the sisters. A blank canvas would be in full view, with a tray of different coloured oil paints, all in the one tray, underneath the canvas. People could bring their own canvas if they wished. The canvas would then be covered by a cloth for anything from around fifteen minutes to sixty minutes. When the cloth was removed a painting was revealed on the canvas; normally a portrait of a deceased loved one, relating to one of the sitters. This was a time when colour photography had not really been developed and one can only imagine the delight of people having a colour painting of their deceased child, husband, mother etc.

However the strange thing was that, although it was oil paints that were in the pots below the canvas, the portraits always looked as though they had been done with pastels. However, the art experts who have examined them say that they are not oil paint, ink or pastel.

They then developed the method of putting two blank canvases together, face to face, and putting them in a window so that the light would stream through; this was reported as giving the canvases a sort of golden glow about them. As before, when the canvases were separated after a sitting, a painting had been produced on one canvas.

They worked in this manner for around thirty years, producing 'who knows how many' paintings. During this time some of the paintings were sent to art experts for analysis. No one could explain just 'how' the paintings were produced as they could find no evidence of brush strokes on the canvas or any other method of paint application. They were then called precipitated art.

It is reported that all of the originals as are fresh today as the day that they were produced, the colour showing no signs of fading. I saw a few of these paintings about fifteen years ago, when Duncan Gascoigne brought them to the SSPR for his lecture at the University of Glasgow. They were certainly very bright and colourful.

Vice-Admiral William Usborne Moore could find no fault with the methodologies of the Bang Sisters. After all of his researches he subsequently wrote a book about all of this called,

Glimpses of the Next State: The Education of An Agnostic.

Chapter 16

QUANTUM THINKING

As if all of these matters are not strange enough, some people postulate that quantum physics may provide us with answers regarding a survival hypothesis. This may or may not be the case. Quantum Physics implies the presence of a wave nature in subatomic particles. The vital difference between a wave and a solid particle is the wave properties of superposition and modulation. Put simply, these properties allow waves of different frequencies to occupy the same space without direct interaction. Therefore, it may be quite possible for parallel universes to exist separated by a difference in some fundamental wave characteristic.

This theory springs directly from wave mechanics which unfortunately was not available to the Victorian researchers when the greatest breakthroughs with mediumship were made.

Even some eminent international physicists postulate that our spirit has a quantum state and that the dualism between our body and soul are just as real as the 'Wave particle dualism' of the smallest particles. At least one former head of the Max Plank Institute for Physics, in Munich, has expressed this opinion.

Do you understand this fully? Me neither, but it seems to show that two 'things' can occupy the same space at the same time and not necessarily interact or be aware of each other. This makes the idea of a 'spirit world' not as crazy as it may once have been.

So...maybe this will prove to be the answer to a 'spirit world', or maybe not.

The famous physicist Neils Bohr said, *Anyone who is not shocked by quantum theory has not understood it.*

Einstein described quantum ideas as, *Spooky action at a distance.*

More quotes on this matter:

I do not like it and I am sorry I ever had anything to do with it.
ERWIN SCHRÖDINGER – SPEAKING OF QUANTUM PHYSICS

But the puzzle is what happened before time began?
DAVID BOHM

The point is that the new raw material doesn't really have to come from anywhere...The universe can start off with zero energy and still create matter.
STEPHEN HAWKING

However, I feel that we all need to heed the following quotation.

The real voyage of discovery consists not in seeking new landscapes but in having new eyes.
MARCEL PROUST

Chapter 17

SCIENCE AND PSI

I will define psi as extrasensory perception, including transfer of information outside generally accepted scientific parameters.

Professor J.B. Rhine's laudable goals were to demonstrate psi, if it existed, in the laboratory in a scientific and strictly controlled manner, and to understand the factors that allowed it to be produced in repeatable experiments anywhere: thereby making the subject respectable as a scientific discipline and hopefully encouraging a flow of funding and a consequent acceleration in our knowledge of the subject by an increase in the number of researchers examining these matters. By bringing statistics into it he also hoped that the judgement of results would be rendered objective and not be a matter of subjective opinion.

Over seventy years of parapsychology has undoubtedly produced a hard, scientific, discipline with results acceptable to any open-minded person who has the scientific training to understand them. To that extent Rhine, his colleagues and his successors did not fail. For example Schmeidler's 'sheep and goats' effect, the 'decline and recovery' effect in performance of card-guessing, the Helmut Schmidt work and the Honorton automated Ganzfeld technique results are, by any scientific standards, capable of being reproduced at will in any laboratory under the prescribed conditions. It can be shown conclusively that none of these results would happen if psi did not exist.

Unfortunately psi-phenomena effects found in the parapsychological laboratory are usually at such weak levels – often called micro-psi – that they are but minnows caught in a fine mesh net of statistics and meta-analysis. It would seem that the cold, rational, calculating, challenging and, dare I say it, the implied 'You're guilty until you prove yourself innocent of fraud' conditions in the sterile parapsychological laboratory are almost guaranteed to numb any ordinary person's psi talent. If spontaneous cases are anything to go by, psi requires the charge of raw emotion and personal involvement to trigger and sustain it. In addition, it is not just the scientific establishment that, in spite of positive results obtained in blind and double blind conditions, still shrugs with parapsychological indifference; it is also the public who do so; in particular the large number of people who are deeply interested in the more traditional psychical research and the answers it might give us about those major questions concerning the nature of human personality. For the most part they have been turned off by parapsychology. For many years the S.P.R. journal, with its high proportion of reports of parapsychological experiments impeccably formulated, carried out and described, but ending in marginal or non-significant results assessed by statistics, became almost unreadable to a high proportion of Society members. It seems fair to say that many former members, previously sympathetic and supportive, were lost to the Society not by death but by boredom. However, I am encouraged by a few of the new breed of parapsychologists who are now getting out and about and dealing with empirical evidence.

I am not suggesting for a moment that we should cease to encourage and support laboratory parapsychology. It is a worthwhile scientific enterprise and has produced unimpeachable statistical evidence supporting the view that human beings can acquire information in ways beyond the five senses. To dismiss this evidence would be to exhibit a severe case of fundamental sceptical blindness. Nonetheless I hope that I have shown in this, and my previous book, that work with powerful mediums and investigations into the other types of cases undertaken previously and in modern times, are at least equally valuable and possibly immensely more productive in gaining insight into the continuing mystery of human personality. By exploring beyond the boundaries of the terrain psyche, we can hopefully attempt to shed some light on what may lie beyond it. After all, our consciousness is still a mystery and no one can really define its source. There are those who say that consciousness is produced by the brain. Dr Deepak Chopra has offered one million dollars to any scientist who can explain how a 'material brain' can produce a single thought. As far as I know, he has not had any claimants thus far.

It is my opinion, and was the opinion of my late colleague Professor Archie Roy, that we disagree strongly with a paper by a parapsychologist (Irwin 2002) who argues that in future it would be sensible for parapsychology to dismiss any attempts to design and carry out 'survival' experiments: such attempts being in his opinion almost certainly a waste of valuable time and funding – there is almost an implication that 'survival' experiments damage the respectability of parapsychology by obliging it to mingle with disreputable neighbours!

Fortunately, and pleasingly, there are signs of a return to the serious study of mediumship in recent years. The S.P.R, London, has a survival research committee specifically devoted to examining problems involved in scientifically studying the possible survival of bodily death. In its lecture programme, two lectures a year – the Gwen Tate Lectures – are specifically slanted towards the survival topic. Under the auspices of the PRISM group of investigators (Psychical Research Involving Selected Mediums), who enjoyed funding from the J.V. Trust and the S.P.R., research work with mediums resulted in three peer reviewed papers. (Robertson and Roy, 2001, Roy and Robertson, 2001 and Robertson and Roy, 2004.) The work that was carried out showed that, using large numbers of participants and mediums and utilising a tight, double blind protocol, highly significant results (statistically) demonstrated the occurrence of paranormal transfer of mediumistic information. Other members of the PRISM group, who studied over a number of years the Scole circle of mediums, (Keen, Fontana and Ellison, 1999) have also produced extremely valuable work greatly enlarging our understanding of working with both physical and mental mediums. In the United States, Professor Gary Schwartz and his group of experimenters continue their productive study of mediumship (Russek, L.G.S., Schwartz, G.E.R., Russek, E. & Russek, H.I., 1999, Schwartz, G.E.R. & Russek, L.G.S., 2001, Schwartz, G.E.R., Russek, L.G.S., Nelson, L.A. & Barentsen, C. 2001, Schwartz, G.E.R., Russek, L.G. & Barentsen, C., 2002), and many more. A fresh approach to mediumship testing is now being undertaken at the Rhine Research Centre in North Carolina, while studies of mediumship have recently been established at the University of Arizona under the title of the William James Post-Doctoral Fellowship; Dr Julie Beischel being the first holder of the post.

Archie and I agreed that traditional psychical research with mediums and the field of spontaneous cases is demonstrably the major way in which significant new progress in our subject will be made: their evidentiality being measured by the court of law criterion of being proven to have occurred beyond a reasonable shadow of doubt. I contend that much too large a proportion of parapsychological work has been devoted to continually re-inventing the wheel of esp. Although, where experienced parapsychologists can point to specific flaws in a particular experiment, efforts should certainly be made to remove such flaws from future experiments. Nevertheless, it must still be said that the designs of many parapsychological experiments in the laboratory and elsewhere seem to be primarily aimed at goals fundamentally chosen so that impeccable planning, unassailable statistical analysis and positive, flawless results will be achieved rather than the possibility that they will provide a chance of making significant progress in understanding human personality. Sadly, such experiments seem as limiting as would be a continuing endeavour to understand the genius of Leonardo da Vinci by analysing repeatedly the chemical composition of the paint in the Mona Lisa.

Chapter 18

THE AFTERLIFE: WHAT MIGHT IT BE LIKE?

Before addressing the idea of how one might spend the time in an afterlife – in fact 'Things we can do when we are dead' – we should take time to clarify just what an afterlife may (or may not) be like.

As I am not dead at the moment, I cannot speak from personal experience and can therefore only look to the reported experiences of others and at seemingly good literature on the matter.

Silver Birch, a corporate intelligence and a spiritual teacher who speaks wisely on many things, explains that different portions of a person's consciousness incarnate at different times. He says:

> There is a consciousness which is you, of which you in the world of matter are expressing but a tiny portion, and there are portions of that same consciousness which are expressing themselves in other spheres of expression. You and the other expressions are all reflections of one inner spiritual reality.

> Try to picture the greater consciousness as a circle and then realise that there are segments of that circle which are revolving around

its centre; when they finally cease to revolve, the different segments occupy their allotted places and the circle is united and complete.

I have also heard this idea described as similar to facets of a diamond. When one life is finished, the experiences that it has endured in that lifetime are taken back to the main "diamond" and added to it to become part of the whole.

When Silver Birch was asked the question, "Does not your explanation of 'split' consciousness express the same truth as F.W.H. Myers's declaration regarding 'group souls?'" The answer was: "It is really the same thing except that it is not a grouping of different souls, but a union of the different portions of consciousness returning to complete the whole."

When asked if two parts of the same "whole" could be incarnated at the same time the answer was, "No that would be contrary to the whole purpose. In each (life experience) you become increasingly conscious of more and more of yourself."

He continued, "It is hard for you to understand because you do not understand what living really means. Life to you has expressed itself practically in its lowest forms. You cannot visualise real life, living intensely in a consciousness that is superior to anything which you can conceive."

Regarding human development on Earth he said:

What you must learn is that there are two forms of development. You can unfold that which is of the soul and you can unfold that which is of the spirit. One is the development of the psychic faculty and the other is soul-growth. Where you get the development of the psychic without the spiritual, there you have a low plane of vibration. When you get a combination of both, then you not only have a great medium, but a great man or woman.

Silver Birch always spoke about 'Natural Law.' He states that the Law is perfect; the soul reaps its own reward and makes its own punishment. The following are answers to questions put to Silver Birch.

Q. Shall we be with those we love in the spirit world, although separated by convention in the physical world?

A. It is impossible to separate love from its beloved.

Q. When we enter the spirit world do we meet relatives who have passed on before?

A. If love exists – yes. If love does not exist – no.

Q. Is the life on the other side everlasting?

A. All life is everlasting, for it belongs to the Great Spirit who is eternal.

Q. Is there only one spirit world.

A. Yes, but it has an infinite number of expressions.

Q. Are the divisions separated in a geographical sense?

A. Not geographically, but in mental scale, which is to some extent conditioned by its physical expression, which effectively means that there are differences for a time until there is evolution beyond that which is conditioned by a physical life.

Let us now look at *The Presence of other Worlds* by Wilson Van Dusen, which examines the work of Emanuel Swedenborg.

Emanuel Swedenborg claimed that he, while still alive, was permitted to walk in heaven and hell. (Which he, incidentally, also described as mental scales)

He speaks about these regions as being extremes of different "levels."

Indeed he proposes that people who claim to speak to the dead are mostly only reaching a very low level – and this level can be quite deceptive.

Swedenborg states that, "Fundamentally, a man's life in these other worlds is based on what he really is. In other words people move toward the essential reality of their existence. It therefore follows that the worlds beyond this one are even more essentially psychological and spiritual than this one. The first state after death is the state of exteriors – everything is the same, people are the same and life is like before.

After a time a person is opened to their real nature and it becomes impossible to act one way and be another."

They are seemingly instructed by friends concerning the state of eternal life. Swedenborg said that the possibility of cheating one's way into heaven dims when the second stage of the spirit world is opened up.

"A person can even go through the opening of the book of lives in which every detail of the life is reviewed. When this is complete a person joins the multitude of others who are essentially at the same 'level'."

'In all respects heaven resembles life on earth – corresponding to earth, there is a government – but those who are given power are those who are of use to others. There are buildings, cities, woods etc. The speech of spirit is not with words, but of ideas, but when they speak with man their speech falls into the words of the man's language.'

Swedenborg says that everyone has work to do within their own level. Heaven is not a place of idleness.

To me this sounds similar to "In my house there are many mansions."

There is no doubt in my mind that sensitives can obtain information from some of these levels. Information which could not possibly be known in any normally accepted way and often outside what we call space and time. It also appears to me that different mediums have such varying ability that they appear to reach different 'levels' and that some can go no further than the initial after death condition.

Psychometry in fact may be just such an example. Oh yes, it works and can work well as a form of information transfer, but does it tell us anything about the afterlife?

Take for example the work of Dr Osty circa 1923 – a French Physician with a deep interest in – and a scientific approach to – psychical research.

There was no doubt left in Osty's mind that this type of information transfer was a fact.

One of the sensitives that he used in his work was Mme. Morel. She worked under hypnosis. Osty obtained a book from M. Boirac, Rector of the Academy of Dijon, for the lady to psychometrise.

"In absolute ignorance of the person whose book this might be I put it in the hands of Mme Morel, hypnotised, asking her to speak of the life of the person to whom it belonged. She said, 'A young man appears to me tall and rather slight. There is nothing characteristic in his appearance but in his eyes, which are not like that of other people. There is nothing wrong with them, but their form is peculiar..... I see this young man for a long while in a place where there is no danger..... He was there with many other men..... Then one day, one morning, he departs with others..... a long march..... then he goes on a train. I see him a little later with others in a kind of hole..... He is standing up with shining eyes..... I hear much noise..... I see fury in his brain; he goes up..... What a noise I hear! He feels a blow and falls..... gets up..... receives another blow and falls afresh with others on a road..... on one side I see grass and cultivated land, on the other side grey mud. He is wounded in the throat and head by a piece of iron."

Two days later this account was sent to M.Boirac, who replied as follows.

"The little manual of Esperanto that I gave you was taken from the civilian clothing left at my house by the son of one of my friends. The young man was a second lieutenant in the 27th regiment, killed or missing on Dec 12th in a trench attack at Bois-Brule. G.M. was aged 26, tall, slight, face rather long and his eyelids had a slight fold like the Chinese, serious and quiet expression..... As far as is known he was wounded leading the attack, but continued at the head of his men, then fell at the edge of the German trench which was still in the hands of the enemy. The first wound seems to have been in the shoulder, the second in his head. The body is supposed to have been taken up by the Germans and buried by them, but there is no certainty. He was returned as "missing." The vision is therefore correct, with some particulars that cannot be ascertained. I can state that the little book was touched by G.M. some months before the scene to which it gave rise."

Therefore this psychometrist correctly described the death conditions of the young man – by touching a small book that belonged to him, *but* the last time the man touched the book, he was alive and well! There are thousands of such accounts which have been carefully examined over many years. All very curious, but does it tell us anything about our existence and a possible afterlife?

In *Conversations with God*, by Neale Donald Walsch, the author asked:

"How does God talk and to Whom?"

The answer received through automatic writing was, "I talk to everyone: all the time. The question is not to whom I talk, but who listens. When we try to speak to each other we are immediately constricted by the unbelievable limitation of words..... for this reason my most common form of communication is through feeling. Feeling is the language of the soul. If you want to know what is true for you, look to how you are feeling about it. I also communicate with thought. Thought and feelings are not the same although they can occur at the same time. Words are really the least effective communicator. They are most open to misinterpretation, most often misunderstood. The highest thought is always that thought which contains joy..... The grandest feeling is that which you call love. Joy, truth and love, these three are interchangeable, and one always leads to the other."

In answer to the question, "Why are we here?" the reply was, "To remember and recreate who you are. The soul, your soul, knows all there is to know – all of the time – yet knowing is not enough – the soul seeks experience. You know that you can be generous but, unless you do something which displays generosity, you have nothing but a concept. You know yourself to be kind but, unless you do someone a kindness, you have nothing but an idea of yourself. It is your soul's desire to turn its grandest concept about itself into its greatest experience."

It has been said that there are only three things in starting a new business: location, location, and location. So what will be the location of your new life and where are you going to be when you pass over? It is quite a thought that we inadvertently sculpture our new state of being when we 'go'.

This would seem to me to tie in with the "mental scale" of existence described by Silver Birch and the "levels" described by Swedenborg.

So the optimist is correct and the pessimist is correct, yet one differs from the other from his own particular point of view. Each is building his world from a particular standpoint which relates to himself. The word Heaven means harmony. The word hell is from old English meaning "to build a wall around, to separate;" to be helled was to be shut off.

To me, all of this makes sense if we look at evidence from some spontaneous cases. Many earthbounds try to cause problems for people still alive, probably because they have locked themselves away in their own particular "hell" – shut off, afraid to move on, scared to let go.

As already discussed, other people who have recently passed seem able to make themselves known to someone on Earth almost immediately by one means or another. E.g. movement of objects, raps, taps electrical disturbances. Their "level" must be such that they can do this.

On The Death of my Son, by a lawyer, Jasper Swain, is a marvellous book. It takes the tragedy of his son's demise from the car crash that caused the death, to the realisation that he can still communicate with him. Jasper asked his son, through a trance medium, "But where are you? What world are you in?"

The reply was, "I'm in a world that looks pretty much the same as your world, Dad; only there are different laws up here..... When I say laws, I don't mean laws that govern the behaviour of people here, I mean laws that govern thought..... While you are still on earth, your thoughts, your intentions, everything that you do, gives your soul a certain rate of vibration. For argument sake, let's suppose your soul is vibrating in a fifty megacycle band. When you die and manifest here, you would go straight to the part of our world which vibrates at fifty megacycles. By the same token, if you're a slow thinking sort of bloke who can only vibrate to fifteen megacycles, then you'll become part of this world in the fifteen megacycle range. Therefore you yourself select the kind of scenery that will await you when you arrive here. The worlds above us are even richer in light and happiness. If I go up there (and I can) I find it too bright; the light hurts my eyes..... so I reverse gear and return to this world – which suits me just fine..... The planes below this one are denser, dimmer planes. If I go down to them it becomes murkier and murkier until it is so creepy that I scoot back here where I belong. This world is the right one for me at this stage of my development; but as my vibrations become more refined, I shall be able to visit the higher planes with ease..... There are many Halls of Knowledge and Wisdom here – you discuss the subject with the lecturer face to face. You can stay all day if you like; except that could be forever, because we have no day or night here." Jasper asked, "Mike, if you are safe in the infinite domain of God; where is hell?" This was met by a burst of hearty laughter. "Gee Dad I'm afraid there's no such place! My Father is a father of love and compassion. He would never permit one of his souls to suffer; and hell would be a place of suffering. I guess it only exists where you are now lovingly preserved in aspic by the sanctimonious!"

So, how do all of the above accounts fit in with our experiences here and now?

For one thing the idea that the lower levels can be deceptive is borne out by a great number of spiritualistic type "circles." So often circle sitters are told that this is going to be the greatest circle of all time – promises, promises and they fizz out within a relatively short time – achieving nothing.

So, what is the afterlife like?

That seems to depend on *you* and the way you live and think in this one.

I would like to add a quote here from the Rt. Rev. Mervyn Stockwood, Lord Bishop of Southwark, as taken from the book *The Woman who Stunned the World, Ena Twigg: Medium*. With reference to life after death he says,

> The Church ought to provide the answer for its followers, but I doubt whether it does, except in a minority of cases. My experience suggests that most priests are ill qualified to provide knowledge, comfort and assurance; instead they content themselves with a routine 'death patter' they picked up in their theological college. My contention is that, if we were to take psychic studies seriously, we would learn to appreciate that our experience in this world is not the consummation; instead we live now *sub specie aeternitatis*. There are other worlds and dimensions and

this should be taught in schools as part of our general education – we must concentrate on psychic studies insofar as they impinge upon our life now and in the future I would hope that it might affect his (man's) values and behaviour in this world, for what is the purpose of survival unless those who survive are prepared for it?

I propose that the preponderance of evidence would tend to suggest that you are a soul within a body, not a body with a soul. Once the 'old glove' of the body has been discarded, the soul still exists with all of its intelligence, motivation, intention and emotion. I feel that this has now been demonstrated and proven in my books as in a court of law, beyond any reasonable doubt, and that once we have passed over there are indeed many, many, *things that we can do when we are dead.*

Two things are infinite: the Universe and human stupidity; and I am not sure about the Universe.

ALBERT EINSTEIN

Chapter 19

TRYING TO MAKE SENSE OF IT ALL

All scientific systems of laws have their limitations. After all, they are merely attempts to summarise as briefly and as accurately as possible the workings of the particular field of nature being studied, and so obtain reliable predictive power within that field. But there is always a sell-by date to any scientific theory or the laws it produces. It is part of the scientific method to test any set of laws to destruction. No true scientist ever sits back and says, "Right, that's it. We know it all. Close the Book of Nature."

It is a matter of public record that innovative scientists and inventors of the past were originally quietly ridiculed for their ideas; for example, Bell and the telephone, the Wright brothers and flight, Benz and the automobile, Eastman for celluloid photographic film, Baird and television, Whittle and the jet engine, Cockerel and the hovercraft; even Watson and Crick were told to drop their study of DNA as the authorities could see no possible use of such research. (How wrong was that?) I have kept these examples simple, as we can all relate to each one, but there are many, many more scientists and inventors who were really hindered by lack of support and funding; however, they plodded on and eventually won the day.

Newton's law of gravitation and his three laws of motion, formulated by him in the seventeenth century, is the prime example of this philosophy. In *The Principia (1687)*, using his four laws and the mathematical tool of differential and integral calculus created by him, he demonstrated that a staggeringly diverse little-understood range of problems now made perfect sense. They included the forms of orbits followed by planets, satellites and comets, the shapes of rotating planets, the precession of the equinoxes, the complex phenomenon of the tides, how to measure the relative masses of the planets, why planets obeyed Kepler's laws, and so on. In the nineteenth century these laws even predicted the existence of a new planet and showed the direction in which a telescope had to be turned to find it. It is not surprising that Alexander Pope wrote his famous couplet:

'Nature and Nature's laws lay hid in night:
God said 'Let Newton be!' and all was light.'

Newtonian celestial mechanics had a spectacularly successful innings before Einstein brought in his theories of relativity in 1905 and 1915, which satisfactorily explained certain small but important anomalies that Newton's laws could not account for. Einstein's theories were formulated from an entirely different viewpoint than that of Newtonian physics. But that is not to say that Newton's laws were scrapped. Relativistic effects are only important when objects travel close to the speed of light (e.g. particles in the Large Hadron Collider) or in a strong gravitational field. Gravitational effects are tiny within the solar system, although (interestingly) they are still measurable. Where the Einstein theories come dramatically into their own and show that Newton is not the only clever kid on the block of science, is exemplified by the case of a pulsar binary, where two rather strange and incredibly dense stars, with regularly pulsating radio outputs, are in close orbit about each other. The nature and sizes of the observed changes in their relative orbit and periods of pulsation are completely predicted by Einstein's theories of relativity whereas Newton's laws fail.

Now it may seem capricious to solemnly formulate a theory involving laws of nature supposed to cover a field of observed data, only to acknowledge that these laws might have to be modified or replaced if some major, or even minor, type of additional phenomena were found for which they cannot account. But that is the name of the scientific game, the most successful game that human beings have ever had.

> Read not to contradict and confute, nor to believe and take for granted,
> but to weigh and consider.
>
> SIR FRANCIS BACON

Just to complicate matters even further, another topic that we do not really understand is that of Time.

In the *Concise Oxford Dictionary,* entries on time occupy one whole page. Very few other topics exceed this amount of space. And yet the direct wordage allocated to the definition of 'time' totals twelve: *Duration, continued existence; progress of this viewed as affecting persons or things.* Not, one must admit, providing us with much in the way of enlightenment regarding the actual nature of time. For such an important subject our understanding of it seems minimal and yet, in every generation, there have been men and women who have wrestled with the subject. Dependent upon their cultural background, their education, their psychical development, each in his, or her, own way has sought an understanding of the nature of time. For some it is an illusion, for others it is a linear process, a convenient mathematical or dynamical device; some have been forced to the conclusion that time is multi-dimensional; modern physicists have introduced the concept of the 'block universe' in which time is but one dimension of a four-dimensional static, unchanging iceberg universe explored by our individual consciousnesses. Special relativity has led some people to conceive of even stranger universes in which time, if it passes, can flow at different rates in different places and may even, for some atomic particles, reverse its direction of flow. Relativity has put elasticity into time's yardstick.

In short, whether we have thought deeply about the matter or not, each one of us has a theory about time, produced by his or her experience of life. Nevertheless St. Augustine really put it in a nutshell when he said, 'When I don't think about time, I understand it perfectly well; it is when I do think about it that I realise I don't understand it at all.'

Most of us go through life without having to think about the nature of time. It is only when something odd occurs that we entertain the suspicion that perhaps things are not quite what they seem.

Perhaps a quick word here about precognition and retrocognition; the former seeing into the future and the latter viewing the past, as if these realities were here and now.

This, I feel, poses several questions, "Are all people who view the past, or future, in an altered state of consciousness and if so why?"

What faculty within a human being allows us to do this?

163

Are we indeed tapping into an archive of the past or future from some block universe which would appear to have no time, or certainly not that which we understand?

Does this make retrocognition a different phenomenon to precognition, or are they two sides of the same coin?

It has been said that there are only two certainties in life, death and taxes. The taxes can take care of themselves and the majority of people don't like to think about death, but as one gets older it seems sensible to investigate this inevitability.

In 1903 Frederic Myers wrote his monumental work *Human Personality and its Survival of Bodily Death* which was posthumously published. Even after all of this time, it remains a work vitally important in connection with our desire to understand the nature of human personality. Perhaps, most important for all of us, is the question of the possible continuance of human personality after physical death. Myers, before he died, claimed that he had been persuaded by his researches that survival takes place. Certainly the Myers communicator via Mrs Piper and Mrs Willett, who gave us the Lethe case, and who was also a prominent communicator in other Cross-Correspondences cases, makes it difficult, if not downright impossible, for anyone of open mind familiar with this evidence not to take it as highly probable that we do in some way survive bodily death. But if so, what is the nature of that survival? The deceased Mrs Willett informed Geraldine Cummins that she was privileged to see her life's file and was also able to meet her daughter, now a young woman, who had died many years previously when she was a young child. Mrs Willett was most surprised to find that they had now nothing in common. Ref. A.E. Roy 'The Eager Dead.'

Indeed there appear to be different kinds of survival. Dependent on the circumstances of our lives and death, as already discussed, we can immediately be comfortable in our new surroundings, choose not to move on immediately, or require help if we linger on as confused earthbounds. Perhaps a modern version of the title of Myers' book, if he were here to rewrite it, would be *Human Personality and the Nature of its Survival of Bodily Death.*

The materialist's belief is that the death of the brain is the total destruction of the person. The consequences of such a belief are:

(a) There is no further existence of a set of personality idiosyncrasies, memories, data, skills, emotional reactions to life events organised and assessed from the Point Of View (POV) of a deceased person.

(b) There is no possibility whatever of a deceased personality directly influencing people who are still alive.

But consider the people who have had interactions with apparitions of all kinds, whether they were solid, semi-transparent or materialisations within a circle. Often these encounters provided previously unknown information to the recipients and the content of that information was organised and delivered from the Point of View (POV) of the deceased.

Let us also consider Professor Ian Stevenson's database:

It contains hundreds (if not thousands) of children who, from when they begin to talk, provide a wealth of details they believe are memories of a previous life, such memories being recalled strictly from the POV of the previous person. There are equally impressive cases studied by many other psychical researchers including Professor Erlendur Haraldsson and Roy Stemman.

Four features in particular are highly significant.

(1) The wealth of details arising from the memories of such a child that enabled a person now dead to be identified.

(2) The high proportion, 65%, of such children who provide a multitude of veridical details unambiguously identifying previous lives cut short. Examples: Swarnlata, Semih Tutus, Purnima Ekanayake,[15] Sonam and many more.

(3) The proportion of children who carry birthmarks not only in the same position but also in the same shape of wounds suffered by violence, accident or illness of the particular person identified by the child's memories.

(4) The number of children providing 'memory' details unambiguously identifying a *living* person whose life experiences match those details. To my knowledge—there are *none*. Surely reminiscent of the significance of 'the dog that did not bark in the night.' (Sherlock Holmes)

Other phenomena which lead me to discount the materialists' beliefs are:

Ostensible 'earthbound' cases, haunts, apparitions and poltergeist cases, which question the nature of the origin of the phenomena. (Hallucinatory, physical or spiritual). Particular cases: Enfield (Guy Lyon

---

[15] Purnima, incense maker – JSPR 64.1, January 2000, pg 20.

Playfair and Maurice Grosse), Maxwell Park (Archie E. Roy and Max Magee), the Cardiff workshop case (Prof. David Fontana), The Rev. Tony Duncan's vicarage, etc.

The transients in the Watseka Wonder and Sumitra possession cases also throw up questions. The people speaking through the 'hosts' had all very recently died.

We must also consider trance mediumship of the calibre of Mrs Piper, Mrs Leonard, Mrs Willett, Mrs Garrett, Miss Cummins, Mr Bjornsson. The Lethe Case (the return of Frederic Myers), the return of George Pelham, the return of Richard Hodgson; 'drop-in' cases – Runki, Gudni Magnusson, Gustav Adolf Biedermann, Harry Stockbridge, the aftermath of the crash of the R101.

Obviously an incomplete but surely thought provoking list.

The present author and Professor Roy spent five years, 1994 - 1999, carrying out an experimental research study on the nature of information given to sitters by mediums. We set out to test the hypothesis that, 'All mediums' statements are so general that they could apply to anyone.'

This study produced a first peer reviewed paper describing the results of a preliminary study. This study did not have a strict protocol applied to it, but sought to find out if there appeared to be any results which would warrant further study. Over a two year period it involved 10 mediums, 44 recipients and 407 non-recipients, the latter being control groups. The results were so outstanding that further research was warranted. JSPR April 2001, pages 91-106.

The second peer reviewed paper described a double blind protocol which would be applied to further research sessions. JSPR July 2001 pages 161-174. It could be argued that some of the conditions were actually triple blind. The experimenter who reduced the data was also blind to the identity of all recipients.

The third peer reviewed paper was published in The JSPR January 2004 pages 18-34. This provided the results of the application of the Robertson-Roy protocol to another series of experiments with mediums which lasted for two and a half years. It involved thirteen sessions, held in a number of locations in Scotland and England, with some 300 participants from a wide variety of cultural backgrounds. A 'set' was normally of the order of 30 statements made to a sole recipient and each medium delivered six sets within a session. Participant audience sizes varied from 25 to 40 people per session. Overall 10 mediums gave 73 sets of statements during these individual sessions. The results showed that even in double blind conditions, the odds against the results being due to chance were one million to one. To date no one has taken up the challenge of replicating this five year study with all of its facets. The conclusion that one is forced to draw from this result is that even without a medium seeing an intended recipient, observing that recipient's body language or hearing ongoing verbal responses, good mediums can make relevant statements to recipients.

At the very least it is a transfer of information from the mediums to recipients, information that the mediums could not possibly have access to by any normally accepted means within our presently accepted scientific paradigms. So where did the information come from?

When asked in later life how he managed to see so much further than others, Newton replied, with commendable modesty, that it was because he had been standing on the shoulders of giants. He was referring to his predecessors such as Copernicus, Galileo and Kepler, who had ascertained the true nature of the orbits of planets and satellites in the solar system and discovered some of the curious relationships between distances from the more massive primaries they orbited and their periods of revolution about their primaries.

Archie Roy and I felt privileged to feel that we were standing on the shoulders of giants of psychical research within our work, for, without the groundwork put in by all of the eminent psychical researchers of the past, probably few people would take us at all seriously. This subject is of prime importance to us all as it may lead us to eventually discover our place in time and space.

At the end of his splendid book *Apparitions*, first published in 1943 and revised and reprinted a number of times, the psychical researcher G.N.M. Tyrrell considered the problem of human personality and survival in the following words.

> Whether psychical research has given reasonable ground for either a positive or negative conclusion regarding survival must, of course, be a matter for individual judgement. It has often been questioned whether positive proof is possible. If I may speak personally, I would say that it seems to me that the crude question has been rubbed off the slate (for the very reason of inadequate background), and instead of a direct answer we have had revealed to us something of the general perspective in which the question ought to be asked. We have shown, in fact, that new conceptions must be grasped before the question can be intelligibly answered. But I think we can say that if the reply had been a simple negative, the vistas of personality now gradually unfolding before us

would not have been found to exist. Psychical Research has certainly not drawn a blank. It has, on the contrary, discovered something so big that people sheer away from it in a reaction of fear. They feel that they cannot cope with it, and are unwilling to make the drastic overhaul of their cherished convictions which the subject demands.

I am totally in agreement with Tyrrell, as was Archie; his words are as relevant today as they were during the Second World War.

And where does that leave us? One century or so after the death of Myers, seventy years after G.N.M. Tyrrell wrote the words quoted above, are we justified in believing that survival in some form, or perhaps in many forms, occurs? If so is it for a limited period of time? Forever? As a file in a cosmic archive that can be downloaded in certain circumstances and activated as a program in the medium's 'computer?' As a conscious, motivated spirit? I am convinced that the vast wealth of evidence gleaned, in the twentieth and twenty-first centuries by just a few dedicated investigators, from the many varieties of paranormal phenomena that exist, have demonstrated with court of law persuasion that bodily death does not totally destroy human personality. In some way that we do not yet understand, the death of a person does leave a non-physical legacy. As I have already said, children remember a previous life, the majority regarding lives that were cut short; people are possessed, displaying completely different personalities; others can be obsessed and, while their own personalities are still present, forced to carry out the unfinished business of the dead, 'drop-ins' gate-crash mediums' trances for their own purposes; a fraction of haunts seem to involve earthbounds of restricted intelligence and confused motivation; while the most successful communicators coming through more than one medium can display personalities that tempt us to believe that they are veritably the surviving spirits of those they claim to be.

I can do no better than leave you with the words of 'an ostensible' Dr Richard Hodgson.

In his life Richard Hodgson began his research into survival as a hard sceptic but, through his experiences and inquiry, his view altered somewhat during the years and after death; while communicating through Mrs Piper, 'he' exhibited extreme ingenuity in striving to overcome the ultra-cautious attitude of those SPR members assessing his true nature, through mediumship. He must have felt that his efforts were falling on deaf ears and eventually took to shouting irritably and in despairing exasperation, "Well, if I am not Hodgson, he never lived!"

Down the decades that cry of the Hodgson communicator still echoes, challenging us all to continue the search for truth and to show that, even if you are just trying to be recognised for who you are, there are indeed things you *can* do when you're dead.

FURTHER READING

Jasbir Lal Jat - *20 Cases Suggestive of Reincarnation* (second edition 1974) Charlottesville, University press of Virginia. I Stevenson.

Lurancy Vennum - R Hodgson, Religio-Philosophical Journal, Dec 20th 1890. JSPR 10, 1901.

A. Roy, *Archives of the Mind*, 1996.S.N.U. Publications.

Sumitra Singh - Stevenson et al 1989, *Journal of Scientific Exploration*, 3,81-101.

Uttara Huddar - VVAkolkar 1992, JASPR, 86,209-247

Thompson/Gifford - Hyslop 1909 PASPR 3, 1-469, A Gauld, PSPR 55 273-340.

Arigo - John G Fuller - *Surgeon of the Rusty Knife* 1974, Readers Union Group.

Purnima, incense maker - JSPR 64.1, January 2000, pg 20.

Chatura Buddika - JSPR 64.. 2 April 2000, Pg 83,84.

Semih Tutusmus - *Children Who Remember a Previous Life*, I. Stevenson, revised edition, 2001.Mcfarland and Co.

Samuel Helander - *Children Who Remember a Previous Life* (as above).

BIBLIOGRAPHY

JSPR/PSPR *Journal/Proceedings of the Society for Psychical Research*

JASPR/PASPR *Journal/Proceedings of the American Society for Psychical Research*

Alexander, E. 2012 *Proof of Heaven. Piatkus 2012*

Braude, S. E. 2003 *Immortal Remains, The Evidence for Life After Death.* Rowman and Littlefield.

Carr, B.J. 2008 Worlds apart: Can psychical research bridge the gulf between matter and mind? PSPR, 59, 1-96.

Cooper, C.2012 *Telephone Calls From the Dead.* Tricorn Books.

Cooper, C. 2013 *Conversations With Ghosts,* White Crow Books

Findlay, Arthur. 1953 *On the Edge of the Etheric, The Rock of Truth, Looking Back, The Way of Life.* WBC Print Ltd.

Fontana, D. 1991 A Responsive Poltergeist: a case from South Wales. *JSPR 57,* 385-403.

Fontana, D. 2009 *Life Beyond Death, What Should We Expect?.* Watkins Publishing.

Fuller, J. G. 1981 *The Airmen Who would not Die,* Corgi, London.

Fuller, J. G. 1974 *Arigo: Surgeon of the Rusty Knife*, Hart-Davis, MacGibbon.

Gauld, A. 1966-72 A Series of 'Drop-in' Communicators, *PSPR 55, 273-340.*

Gauld, A. 1968 *The Founders of Psychical Research.* London: Routledge and Kegan Paul.

Gauld, A. and Cornell, A.D.1979 *Poltergeists. London and Boston:* Routledge & Kegan Paul.

Gauld, A. 1982. *Mediumship and Survival.* Heinemann, London.

Gurney, E., Myers, F. W. H., and Podmore, F1886.*Phantasms of the Living,* vols. 1 and 2. The Society for Psychical Research and Trubner and Company.

Hamilton, T. 2012 *Tell My Mother I'm not Dead.* Imprint Academic.

Haraldsson, E. 2000 Birthmarks and Claims of Previous-Life Memories. 1. The Case of Purnima Ekanayake. *JSPR, 64.1, 16-25.*

Haraldsson, E. 2013 *The Departed Among The Living.* White Crow Books.

Haraldsson, E. and Stevenson, I. 1975, A Communicator of the 'Drop-in' type in Iceland: The Case of Runolfur Runolfsson. *JASPR 69, 35-59.*

Haraldsson, E. and Stevenson, I. 1975, A Communicator of the 'Drop-in' type in Iceland: The Case of Gudni Magnusson. *JASPR 69, 245-261.*

Hutton J. B. 1978 *Healing Hands.* W.H. Allen.

Hyslop, J. H. 1909. A Case of Veridical Hallucinations, *PASPR 3, 1-469.*

Inglis, Brian. 1977 *Natural and Supernatural,* Hodder and Stoughton.

Inglis, Brian. 1984 *Science and Parascience,* Hodder and Stoughton.

Inglis, Brian. 1985 *The Paranormal,* Granada, London.

Ireland, M. 2010 *Soul Shift.* Frog Books.

Ireland, M. 2013 *Messages From The Afterlife,* North Atlantic Books, California.

Lodge, O. 1909 *Survival of Man,* Methuen, London.

Lodge, O. 1911 Evidence of Classical Scholarship and of Cross-Correspondence in some New Automatic Writing. *PSPR 25,129-142.*

Mackenzie, A. 1971 *Apparitions and Ghosts.* Arthur Barker, London.

Peake, A. 2010, *Is There Life after Death?* Arcturus Publishing Ltd.

Piper, A. L. 1929 *The Life and Work of Mrs. Piper.* London: Kegan Paul.

Playfair, G. L. 2011 *This House is Haunted,* White Crow Books, Guildford.

Playfair, G. L. and Grosse, M. 1988 Enfield Revisited, *JSPR 55, 50-78.*

Playfair, G. L. 2012 *Twin Telepathy.* White Crow Books, Guildford.

Playfair, G. L. 2011 *Chico Xavier, Medium of the Century.* Roundtable publishing.

Psychic Press. 1979 *The Teachings of Silver Birch*

Richet, C. 1923. *Thirty Years of Psychical Research: Being a Treatise on Metapsychics* (S. de Brath, Trans.) New York: MacMillan.

Robertson T. J. 2013, *Things You Can Do When You're Dead,* White Crow Books.

Robertson T. J. and Roy *A.E.*2001, A preliminary Study of the Acceptance by Non-Recipients of Mediums' Statements to Recipients. *JSPR 65.2 91-106*

Roy A. E. and T. J Robertson 2001, A Double Blind Procedure for assessing The Relevance of a Medium's Statements to a Recipient .*JSPR 65.3 161-74*

Robertson T. J. and Roy A. E. 2004, Results of the Application of the Robertson-Roy Protocol to a series of Experiments with Mediums and Participants. *JSPR 68.1 18-34*

Rogo, D. Scott, 1979 *The Poltergeist Experience.* Penguin books, Baltimore (USA).

Rogo, D. Scott, 1988 *The Infinite Boundary.* The Aquarian Press: Wellingborough.

Roy, A.E. 1996 *The Archives of the Mind.* Psychic Press, Stansted.

Roy, A.E. 2008 *The Eager Dead,* Book Guild.

Sartori, P. 2014 *The Wisdom of Near-Death Experiences,* Watkins.

Stemman, R. 2012 *The Big Book Of Reincarnation,* Hierophant Publishing.

Stevenson, I. Are Poltergeists Living or are They Dead? 1972 *JASPR66, 233 - 252.*

Stevenson, I. 1974 *Twenty Cases Suggestive of Reincarnation,* University of Virginia Press, Charlottesville.

Stevenson, I. 1975 *Cases of the Reincarnation Type. Vol. 1. Ten Cases in India.* Charlottesville: University Press of Virginia.

Stevenson, I. 1977 *Cases of the Reincarnation Type. Vol. 2. Ten Cases in Sri Lanka.* Charlottesville: University Press of Virginia.

Stevenson, I. 1980 *Cases of the Reincarnation Type. Vol. 3. Twelve Cases in Lebanon and Turkey.* Charlottesville: University Press of Virginia.

Stevenson, I. 1987 *Children Who Remember Previous Lives.* Charlottesville:

Swain, J. 1983 *On the Death of My Son.* Turnstone Press Ltd

University Press of Virginia.

Tucker, J. 2014 *Return to Life.* St Martin's Press, New York

Twigg E. 1973 *The Woman Who Stunned The World,* Manor Books Inc.

Wilson, C. 1982 *Poltergeist,* New English Library, London.

Zammit, V and W. 2013 *A Lawyer Presents the Evidence for the Afterlife.* White Crow Books

ABOUT THE AUTHOR

A former teacher of mathematics and physics, Tricia is a long-term council member, past Vice President and Immediate Past President of the Scottish Society for Psychical Research.

She was a tutor for the Department of Adult and Continuing Education (DACE) at the University of Glasgow. In conjunction with Professor Archie Roy she provided a session programme of 20, 2 hour, lectures per session for DACE in a series entitled "An In Depth Study of Psychical Research." This course ran for six years examining: The paranormal – what is the evidence?'

In addition to 30 years of experience in investigating spontaneous cases Tricia has appeared on various TV programmes, usually documentaries, on various people's blogs and on radio programmes including America's *Coast to Coast,* UK's Radio City, Celtic Radio and the unexplainedtv.com and has been invited, over many years, to speak to varied organisations throughout the U K.

Her first book achieved a ranking of 529 at one point on Amazon.com.

She has written the forward to Dr Mark Ireland's highly successful book *Soul Shift* and has text included in his book *Messages from the Afterlife,* written an endorsement for *The Galilean Pendulum* and some of her comments are on the back cover of Trevor Hamilton's book *Tell my Mother I am not Dead.*

She has a wealth of experience in investigating spontaneous cases and has done so for around 30 years. Tricia is known as an interesting speaker on many topics concerning psychical research, which is reflected by the invitations that she receives from varied avenues.

Lectures in recent years include:

Various plus The 'Gwen Tate' Lecture for the SPR in London, in October 2005

The Glastonbury Symposium 2006

SPR Study Day presentation 2006

The Ghost Club, London, 2006

The Theosophical Society of Edinburgh, 2005

The Churches Fellowship for Psychic and Spiritual Studies- on various occasions

The Edinburgh College of Parapsychology – various occasions

The Ayrshire Association for Spiritual Knowledge – yearly since 1989 to June 2008

Muncaster Castle Conference 2004

The Lynwood Fellowship – various occasions

Stirling association of spiritual knowledge – various occasions last one Sept 2008

The West of Scotland Dowsers – various occasions

Presidential Address for the SSPR 2005

Unitarian Church, Glasgow 2005, 2006,2007,2008

A lecture to Mensa at Malvern 2006

Lecture to A.S.K , Dreghorn, June 2009

A Gwen Tate Lecture for the SPR London October 2009

Norwegian Parapsychological Soc. 2010

Lecture to Quakers in Oxford Oct 2010

Invited speaker to the International conference of the London based SPR 2011

Invited speaker at SPR Study Day 2012

Speaker for West of Scotland Dowsers 2013

Speaker for Arthur Conan Doyle Centre 2013

Invited speaker for SPR Study Day 2013

West of Scotland Dowsers January 2014

Stirling spiritualist Church April 2014.

Speaker Arthur Conan Doyle Centre Edinburgh May 2014

Inverclyde Seminar October 2014

Speaker SSPR November 2014.

Glasgow University Ladies Club January 2015
Further speaking dates have also been booked for 2015 and 2016.

Research

Along with many television appearances, normally in documentaries, since 1990 she has also prepared and presented many papers to the SPR International Conferences, over the past 20 years.

She is the co-author, with Professor Archie Roy, of three published papers on the study of information provided by mediums. These papers follow a five-year study of controlled experiments in conditions up to triple blind. The results of these studies are published in the JSPR April 2001, January 2004 and July 2004.

Tricia was a founding member, and Hon Sec of PRISM, Psychical Research Involving Selected Mediums, 1994 - 2008.

She has also completed a four/five year, in depth, study of exceptional paranormal healing, which started 2006 and produced some spectacular results. Some of these results are suggestive of some form of psychic surgery. The final report may be downloaded from her website www.triciarobertson.weebly.com

She has completed a report on a 6 year old boy in Scotland, who remembers a previous life.

Apart from three published peer reviewed papers in the JSPR, she has articles published in many journals including the journals of the Swedish and Norwegian Societies for Psychical Research.

Tricia is passionate about the evidence gathered in various aspects of Psychical Research, and does not suffer gladly fools who will not address specific evidence in any particular avenue.

While accepting that some people may be deluded in some aspects of experience, it is absolutely certain that there are genuine cases in nearly every aspect of paranormal claims and that the evidence for survival of human personality is undeniable for those who really want to examine these matters with an unbiased mind.

Paperbacks also available from
White Crow Books

Elsa Barker—*Letters from
a Living Dead Man*
ISBN 978-1-907355-83-7

Elsa Barker—*War Letters from
the Living Dead Man*
ISBN 978-1-907355-85-1

Elsa Barker—*Last Letters from
the Living Dead Man*
ISBN 978-1-907355-87-5

Richard Maurice Bucke—
Cosmic Consciousness
ISBN 978-1-907355-10-3

Arthur Conan Doyle—
The Edge of the Unknown
ISBN 978-1-907355-14-1

Arthur Conan Doyle—
The New Revelation
ISBN 978-1-907355-12-7

Arthur Conan Doyle—
The Vital Message
ISBN 978-1-907355-13-4

Arthur Conan Doyle with
Simon Parke—*Conversations
with Arthur Conan Doyle*
ISBN 978-1-907355-80-6

Meister Eckhart with Simon Parke—
Conversations with Meister Eckhart
ISBN 978-1-907355-18-9

D. D. Home—*Incidents in my Life Part 1*
ISBN 978-1-907355-15-8

Mme. Dunglas Home; edited,
with an Introduction, by Sir
Arthur Conan Doyle—*D. D.
Home: His Life and Mission*
ISBN 978-1-907355-16-5

Edward C. Randall—
Frontiers of the Afterlife
ISBN 978-1-907355-30-1

Rebecca Ruter Springer—
Intra Muros: My Dream of Heaven
ISBN 978-1-907355-11-0

Leo Tolstoy, edited by Simon
Parke—*Forbidden Words*
ISBN 978-1-907355-00-4

Leo Tolstoy—*A Confession*
ISBN 978-1-907355-24-0

Leo Tolstoy—*The Gospel in Brief*
ISBN 978-1-907355-22-6

Leo Tolstoy—*The Kingdom
of God is Within You*
ISBN 978-1-907355-27-1

Leo Tolstoy—*My Religion:
What I Believe*
ISBN 978-1-907355-23-3

Leo Tolstoy—*On Life*
ISBN 978-1-907355-91-2

Leo Tolstoy—*Twenty-three Tales*
ISBN 978-1-907355-29-5

Leo Tolstoy—*What is Religion
and other writings*
ISBN 978-1-907355-28-8

Leo Tolstoy—*Work While
Ye Have the Light*
ISBN 978-1-907355-26-4

Leo Tolstoy—*The Death of Ivan Ilyich*
ISBN 978-1-907661-10-5

Leo Tolstoy—*Resurrection*
ISBN 978-1-907661-09-9

Leo Tolstoy with Simon Parke—
Conversations with Tolstoy
ISBN 978-1-907355-25-7

Howard Williams with an Introduction
by Leo Tolstoy—*The Ethics of Diet:
An Anthology of Vegetarian Thought*
ISBN 978-1-907355-21-9

Vincent Van Gogh with Simon Parke—
Conversations with Van Gogh
ISBN 978-1-907355-95-0

Wolfgang Amadeus Mozart with Simon
Parke—*Conversations with Mozart*
ISBN 978-1-907661-38-9

Jesus of Nazareth with Simon Parke—
Conversations with Jesus of Nazareth
ISBN 978-1-907661-41-9

Thomas à Kempis with Simon
Parke—*The Imitation of Christ*
ISBN 978-1-907661-58-7

Julian of Norwich with Simon
Parke—*Revelations of Divine Love*
ISBN 978-1-907661-88-4

Allan Kardec—*The Spirits Book*
ISBN 978-1-907355-98-1

Allan Kardec—*The Book on Mediums*
ISBN 978-1-907661-75-4

Emanuel Swedenborg—*Heaven and Hell*
ISBN 978-1-907661-55-6

P.D. Ouspensky—*Tertium Organum:
The Third Canon of Thought*
ISBN 978-1-907661-47-1

Dwight Goddard—*A Buddhist Bible*
ISBN 978-1-907661-44-0

Michael Tymn—*The Afterlife Revealed*
ISBN 978-1-970661-90-7

Michael Tymn—*Transcending the
Titanic: Beyond Death's Door*
ISBN 978-1-908733-02-3

Guy L. Playfair—*If This Be Magic*
ISBN 978-1-907661-84-6

Guy L. Playfair—*The Flying Cow*
ISBN 978-1-907661-94-5

Guy L. Playfair —*This House is Haunted*
ISBN 978-1-907661-78-5

Carl Wickland, M.D.—
Thirty Years Among the Dead
ISBN 978-1-907661-72-3

John E. Mack—*Passport to the Cosmos*
ISBN 978-1-907661-81-5

Peter & Elizabeth Fenwick—
The Truth in the Light
ISBN 978-1-908733-08-5

Erlendur Haraldsson—
Modern Miracles
ISBN 978-1-908733-25-2

Erlendur Haraldsson—
At the Hour of Death
ISBN 978-1-908733-27-6

Erlendur Haraldsson—
The Departed Among the Living
ISBN 978-1-908733-29-0

Brian Inglis—*Science and Parascience*
ISBN 978-1-908733-18-4

Brian Inglis—*Natural and Supernatural:
A History of the Paranormal*
ISBN 978-1-908733-20-7

Ernest Holmes—*The Science of Mind*
ISBN 978-1-908733-10-8

Victor & Wendy Zammit —*A Lawyer
Presents the Evidence For the Afterlife*
ISBN 978-1-908733-22-1

Casper S. Yost—*Patience
Worth: A Psychic Mystery*
ISBN 978-1-908733-06-1

William Usborne Moore—
Glimpses of the Next State
ISBN 978-1-907661-01-3

William Usborne Moore—
The Voices
ISBN 978-1-908733-04-7

John W. White—
The Highest State of Consciousness
ISBN 978-1-908733-31-3

Stafford Betty—
The Imprisoned Splendor
ISBN 978-1-907661-98-3

Paul Pearsall, Ph.D. —
Super Joy
ISBN 978-1-908733-16-0

**All titles available as eBooks, and selected titles available in Hardback and
Audiobook formats from www.whitecrowbooks.com**

Lightning Source UK Ltd.
Milton Keynes UK
UKOW03f0809250417
299847UK00004B/233/P